£3

18/40.

Support systems in social work

Library of Social Work

General Editor:
Noel Timms
Professor of Social Work Studies
University of Newcastle upon Tyne

Support systems in social work

Martin Davies

School of Social Studies
University of East Anglia

Routledge & Kegan Paul
London, Henley and Boston

First published in 1977
by Routledge & Kegan Paul Ltd
39 Store Street,
London WC1E 7DD,
Broadway House,
Newtown Road,
Henley-on-Thames,
Oxon RG9 1EN and
9 Park Street,
Boston, Mass. 02108, USA
Set in 10 on 11pt English
and printed in Great Britain by
The Lavenham Press Limited
Lavenham, Suffolk

British Library Cataloguing in Publication Data

Davies, Martin, b. 1936

Support systems in social work. —(Library of
social work).

1. Support Project—History
I. Title   II. Series
361.7'09427'33   HV250.M2   77-30005

ISBN 0-7100-8616-4
ISBN 0-7100-8617-2 Pbk

For Judy, Andrew and Paul—Support System Extraordinary

Contents

Preface

At a time when social work is becoming simultaneously more all-embracing and yet increasingly geared to highly specific functions of decision making, resource allocation, prevention and social control, the traditional helping mode has become both unfashionable and over-shadowed by current controversies. This short book is not designed as a comprehensive review of the concept of 'helping', but it is, nevertheless, that concept which runs through the text and which is constantly pointed to as an element of some significance.

The book effectively comprises three self-contained, but linked, parts. The link is provided by a modest experiment in voluntary service carried out in Manchester between 1971 and 1974. The parts were written as a result of the author's association with the experiment, although they each have a different emphasis and, to some extent, were designed for different audiences.

Part one, contained in chapters 1 and 2, was first drafted in 1974 and describes the history and development of the Support Project from the perspective of its sponsors and their organiser. It raises questions about the legitimacy of the Project's objectives and draws attention to some of the implications of the way in which it was designed.

Part two, contained in chapters 3 to 6, introduces material reflecting the perspectives of the volunteers and the families to which they were allocated. It also briefly touches on the attitudes of the headmasters who were responsible for using the volunteers and casts a sideways glance at the Social Services Department, whose short-comings as a helping agency were frequently alleged to have made the use of volunteers essential. The interviews which form the basis for this essay were mainly carried out in the summer of 1974 and they are intended to provide a more rounded and, therefore, necessarily more complex view of what the Support Project had achieved.

Part three follows up earlier work (Davies, 1974, pp. 95-100) in which the author used theoretical perspectives from systems thinking to clarify the role and function of social workers. In chapters 7 and 8, systems theory is interpreted for its applicability to social work, and the concepts, as they are introduced, are illustrated by direct reference to the Support Project. Conclusions are drawn which have major significance for the practice and organisation of the personal social services.

The three parts are presented in ascending order of complexity. The first is straightforward and to some extent naive; the second, closely reflecting the contrasting aspects of human interaction, contains paradoxes and some uncertainty and illustrates the conflicting perspectives of client and worker; the third part explicitly acknowledges the legitimacy of paradox, uncertainty and conflict in social life and suggests that no welfare policy can ignore their presence. It may be that social work will have to acknowledge the increasing demands of society that its practitioners should function with greater precision and with more measurable success. To the extent that that is so, however, there will emerge an immense gap in our society's provisions for human welfare, a gap that remains to be filled by those offering counselling, pastoral care, help, support, watchfulness. Our civilised urban society must now begin to meet the need by utilising the depth of volunteer commitment that exists in every street, neighbourhood, tower block and lodging house, but rarely tapped in some areas because of the breakdown in communication networks which characterises much city life.

For three years the author enjoyed happy association with all the headmasters, volunteers and associated workers in the Support Project; he is grateful for their friendship, their interest and their stimulating ideas. Funds from the Department of Health and Social Security, from the National Elfrida Rathbone Society and from the Manchester Council for Voluntary Service were essential to the Project's survival, and the MCVS, in particular, provided the resources which enabled the monitoring exercise reported in the first essay to be completed. The Nuffield Foundation made available a generous grant to enable the fieldwork for the research reported in the second essay to be completed, and a succession of students on the two-year social work course in the Department of Social Administration at Manchester University helped the author by their criticisms and comments to prepare the third essay in its present form.

Four individuals deserve a special word of gratitude. Emily White was the General Secretary of the MCVS throughout the time of the author's association with the Project and her encouragement and commitment have ensured that it could be recorded in such a way that the lessons learnt from it might be passed on to others similarly engaged. Sheila Worthington was the organiser throughout the period to which this book refers and her friendliness, warmth and good temper enabled the author, in his role as research worker, to carry out his task successfully. Paul Slight worked hard for three months in the summer of 1974 undertaking the greater part of the fieldwork recorded in the second essay. He was able to draw on the experiences of both volunteers and families and to work with the author in determining their relevance for the emergent theme. And Sue Barlow worked with the author in preparing the final manuscript and typed it quickly and efficiently. Without these four colleagues the study could not have been completed successfully, and the author extends his gratitude to them.

Monitoring the Support Project

Chapter one

The Project

Introduction

For three years from 1971, the Manchester Council for Voluntary Service, in association with the National Elfrida Rathbone Society and with the financial support of the Department of Health and Social Security, administered a project in which volunteers provided support for selected children from Manchester's special schools and their families. Most of these schools are for children with learning difficulties—a phrase which has replaced the traditional term *educationally subnormal*, on the grounds that it is both less stigmatising and more accurate, because of the wide range of social and psychological factors which may lie behind the fact that a child is failing to respond to the educational process.

Some children at special schools enjoy supportive home backgrounds, sympathetic parents and adequate material resources; but many do not and, for them, the problems of coping with an increasingly complex urban society are aggravated not only by their learning difficulties but also by the stresses attendant upon their home life. For these children, the Support Project was established.

The work of the special schools is characterised by small classes, imaginative teaching and a particular emphasis on home-school liaison; despite this, the staff find they are unable to give the out-of-school attention to their pupils they feel some children need and, although many of the families are already known to the Social Services Department or to probation officers, it was felt there was an evident need to offer them more support on a regular basis. Perhaps the answer lay in recruiting volunteers to befriend the children and their parents, to offer them guidance and to help them through times of crisis.

3

Chapters 1 and 2 of this book provide an assessment of the Support Project, indicate its shortcomings and achievements and inevitably highlight some of the general issues that surround the emerging question—what function is the volunteer to perform in contemporary society? The notion of voluntary effort spans a wide range of activity: at one extreme, there is a long middle-class tradition of direct intervention by the cultural outsider into another's life-situation with a view to improving it; and, at the other, there is a more recent pattern in which self-help groups have been encouraged to work at grass-roots level in the community. It is immediately apparent that the Support Project belongs to the traditional genre, and it is important to emphasise that the writer has no advance commitment to the superiority of either approach. It is, however, clear that the answers to questions about the volunteer's role are of crucial importance to a great many welfare organisations—both voluntary and statutory—as they plan their future strategy.

The Project could not be evaluated experimentally. Such an approach would have been inappropriate, unwelcome (because of the inevitable intrusions that would have been made into the work of the schools, the organiser and the volunteers) and methodologically unsound. The report is based partly on a monitoring exercise governed by research criteria, partly on interviews with participants and the conclusions drawn have been carefully checked against the available evidence. The focus in chapters 1 and 2 is on practice and administration, and in chapters 3 to 6 on the participants' experience of the Project.

Origins and development of the Project

The Project was justified throughout its life in terms of a simple assertion made at the outset: children with learning difficulties have a self-evident need for 'a great deal of help and support both in and out of school'. There were two strands to the argument:

(a) because of a lack of self-confidence and inadequate social competence, there is a marked need for support at the time when a child transfers from a special school to work;
(b) but there is also a more general need for support in the home during the time that a child is at a special school, because of the inadequacy of many of the families and the consequent hindrance to the child's school performance.

Origins

In 1968, the MCVS* was anxious to decide on new areas into which it could extend its social service operations and, in December, a meeting was held with the Rathbone Society at which interest was expressed in the use of volunteers to befriend ESN school-leavers in order to help them 'make the transition from school to work'.

In November 1969, a pilot scheme was implemented at Park and Woodside Schools in Wythenshawe. Ten volunteers were recruited, attended a training session, and eight were allocated to the youth clubs in the two schools. 'Having visited the clubs fairly regularly for some months, the volunteers began to make home visits—usually introduced in the first instance by the school counsellor.' The emphasis of this scheme was intended to be on the problems faced by school-leavers.

In October 1970, Riverside School in Didsbury launched its own scheme for the use of volunteers, and here the emphasis was on the provision of casework support for the families of children still at the school: 'if the child is really to derive benefit from the special educational treatment offered in school then he also needs support out of school in his home environment'. At Riverside, the volunteers were introduced to families by the home-school liaison teacher, and it was intended that they should be able to get help and advice either from the school or from a child care officer who had expressed interest in the scheme.

Many social workers have recognised—most notably in the probation service—that volunteers do not save time, they take time: to recruit, to train, to organise and to supervise; and although they can be a valuable additional resource, it is short-sighted to imagine that they will not make demands on the existing structure. Indeed, it was quickly recognised by the headmasters at Park, Riverside and Woodside Schools that the use of volunteers was making demands on their own time and on that of their teaching staff which might grow to such an extent that they could outweigh the value of the volunteers' work with children and their families. Neither the schools nor the voluntary societies could provide the concentration of effort necessary for the maintenance and development of the scheme, and in November 1970, it had been decided that the MCVS should be responsible for appointing an organiser. Early in 1971, the DHSS agreed to back the scheme for a period of three years, and both the voluntary bodies involved also committed themselves to giving some financial support.

*During the course of the Project, the Manchester and Salford Council of Social Service has become the Manchester Council for Voluntary Service. This report uses the new name throughout.

The Project

In the discussions that took place before the launching of the new scheme, the persistence of the two strands could clearly be seen, and the background to the Support Project can be summarised diagrammatically. (See Figure 1.1.)

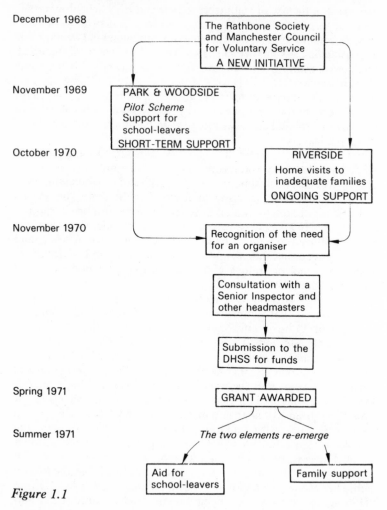

Figure 1.1

Development
In September 1971 the appointed part-time organiser took up her post and began work, and in the following month the operational pattern was outlined by one of the headmasters at a meeting of the Project's Advisory Group:

6

(a) the family will be chosen by the school;

(b) the volunteers' organiser will be approached and asked to find a suitable volunteer;

(c) the volunteer will be interviewed by the headmaster and then introduced by the headmaster or his representative to the family;

(d) there will be monthly report meetings, with a representative of the Social Services Department present;

(e) a written report will be submitted by the volunteer to the school;

(f) if the volunteer has difficulty in attending meetings, the organiser will visit him at home.

This pattern emphasised the crucial role of the headmasters and their ultimate responsibility for any matters affecting the care of their schoolchildren. As the Project developed, the pattern showed a number of variations from that proposed:

(a) and (b) the chronological order was reversed. The normal procedure was for the organiser to recruit volunteers and then to approach the headmasters to see if they could identify a suitable child or family. This reversal simply reflected the supply-and-demand situation of the scheme: it was easier to identify a family in need than it was to find a volunteer, and in so far as matching took place, it was dependent on the availability of a suitable volunteer;

(c) The volunteers were all interviewed by the headmasters, who retained the power of veto over the selections made by the organiser; in practice, however, the developing skill of the organiser was such that her decisions were almost always supported by the headmasters. The introduction of a volunteer to a family was usually made by a teacher, with the organiser present on occasions;

(d) meetings were not held monthly, but held each term. The representative of the Social Services Department attended;

(e) written reports were not requested or produced;

(f) the organiser maintained *regular* telephone or personal contact with volunteers, not only as a result of their failure to attend meetings.

The main characteristic of the scheme as it evolved was its dependence on a close working relationship between the headmasters and the organiser, and this pattern led to the organiser becoming the keystone of its failure or success, with the headmasters largely dependent on her, not only for recruitment but also for the supervision of volunteers.

The work of the Project continued on an even keel throughout the first three years' operation. The sections that follow describe various aspects of its progress, but three points need to be made at the outset:

(a) The two strands continued throughout the period. There were recurring emphases on the needs of school-leavers and on the longer-term needs of inadequate families for support from the volunteers. In practice, however, only a small number of school-leavers were reached in the way that was originally intended in the Wythenshawe Pilot Scheme. This may be partly because the Advisory Group in its early decisions and the Project organiser in her publicity, tended to emphasise the befriending aspect of the volunteers' work, but it is more probable that this policy was adopted because there was an intuitive realisation of the difficulties inherent in the idea of employing volunteers to use crisis intervention techniques to help school-leavers overcome the problems of starting work. The difficulties are twofold: first, in order to offer help in a difficult situation, the volunteer has to be trusted, and in order to be trusted, it is essential for there to be time in which the relationship can develop; and second, as will be seen, the so-called 'short-term' volunteers were not really 'short-term' at all and it was not appropriate to use them for crisis support in the way that had been intended. Accordingly it was hoped that volunteers attached to families on a long-term basis would be in a position to help the school-leaver when the problem arose—two, three or more years hence.

   This is not to argue that a voluntary advice service could not be provided for the school-leaver, but that the relatively unstructured befriending approach of the Support Project did not prove to be appropriate for this purpose. In order to establish a suitable service, there would have to be a clearer appreciation of the kind of aid needed, and closer liaison with the Government departments concerned. The Support Project, generally speaking, adopted a policy of providing family support no matter what stage the child was at in his school or afterwards.

(b) An early policy assertion was made that the volunteers would not be employed with families who were already in touch with professional social workers. Instead it was hoped that they would be allocated to families 'who are not recognised social problems' but who might become such if they did not receive support. In practice this distinction proved impossible to maintain, and in the vast majority of cases, the families supported were known to one or more of the social services. This is because those children felt by their headmasters to be most in need of support were those with severe family difficulties; and the original plan could be adhered to only if the headmasters had been confident that social workers were already providing the kind of intensive support that they felt was needed in order to enable the child to take advantage of his school education. In most cases, such support from the statutory services was quite impracticable. Accordingly the volunteers not only worked with families well known to the professionals, but in some cases were allocated to situations which would make many a social worker quail.

(c) Throughout the period, no specific pattern of training was adopted, and applicants were not required to undertake any minimal course-work, although regular meetings were held at which speakers raised social services topics and provided an opportunity for discussion. In addition, it was suggested to some volunteers that they might attend courses run by the University Extra-Mural Department.

A general review
The Support Project was not spectacular in the way that many community projects are. In the words of Peter Nokes, its emphasis was not on virtuoso performances as a result of which major changes are brought about in peoples' behaviour or circumstances, but on the often over-looked need for *general care.* The very name of the Project recognised this, and was unusually apt: the volunteers were asked to give *support,* and they were encouraged to go on doing so even when they doubted the effectiveness of their work.

The qualities of the Project are similarly low-key:
(a) it was not established in a hurry: it was conceived three years before it was launched, and grew slowly and steadily;
(b) the focus was on action, with virtually no superfluous energy spent on the kinds of trimmings that often tempt voluntary organisations;
(c) the Project was not committed to over-ambitious goals of the kinds some government-sponsored projects have had to accept. There was a simple outline of need, and a plan of action which required only that the Project should recruit and supervise people who might meet that need;

(d) the organiser had no responsibilities beyond those involved in running the Project, and the scale of the operation was such that there had to be little in the way of organisational super-structure;

(e) inevitably, there were potential traps but these seemed to be by-passed successfully;

(f) all the participants in the Project contributed to its success—the MCVS and its Volunteers' Organiser, the headmasters and teaching staff of the schools, and above all, the organiser herself; her role will be discussed in detail later. One factor is of undoubted importance: during a project of this kind continuity can be crucial and the fact that the organiser stayed with the Project for its initial three-year span was a major stabilising factor.

The work of the Project is summarised in Figure 1.2. At the top is the butterfly relationship between the schools and the volunteers, with the organiser linking the two together; her relationship with both was crucial. But having formed the link, the school identified a family, the volunteer was introduced, and the work of the volunteer with the family then assumed semi-independence. The volunteer worked on his own, conferring with the organiser or school as need arose or in response to the organiser's or school's initiative. On rare occasions, the volunteer reverted to an identification with the school if it appeared to be appropriate, or if there was an insistent demand for role clarification; but for the most part it seemed he deliberately left his role and status cloudy.

Some facts and figures

In October 1971, when the Support Project's organiser took up her post, there were three volunteers on the books as a result of the pilot work undertaken earlier. One of these continued to serve until May 1973; by January 1974 another was still working with a family she had known for three years; the third had never been allocated to a family, but undertook a variety of jobs in one of the schools, and she, too, was still functioning when the statistical analysis was completed.

With these exceptions, the organiser began from scratch in 1971; by 1 January 1974, she had been responsible for recruiting seventy-eight volunteers. Figure 1.3 summarises the pattern of recruitment and service. There was a rapid build-up in the first three months of the Project, and the list topped thirty for the first time by April 1972. It then dropped until the autumn, when it started to recover to reach a second peak in March to May 1973. There was again a fall during the summer, but it was less severe, and recovered more quickly, so that the list was re-established at thirty-plus by October 1973. Figure 1.4 summarises the trend by showing mean list figures for each quarter, 1971-3.

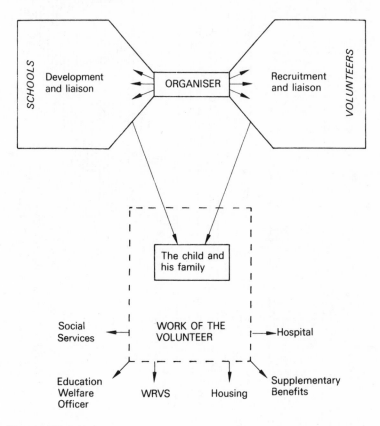

Figure 1.2

The relatively severe fall-back in the current list during 1972 may have been linked to the fact that there was a minor crisis of morale in the Project at that time because of difficulties in securing funds to provide adequate research and consultancy facilities to the organiser. However, it is clear from an examination of the total period that, much more significantly, there was a recurring problem of recruitment during the summer months and that the effects of this in 1972 were probably aggravated by the relatively high wastage of volunteers

11

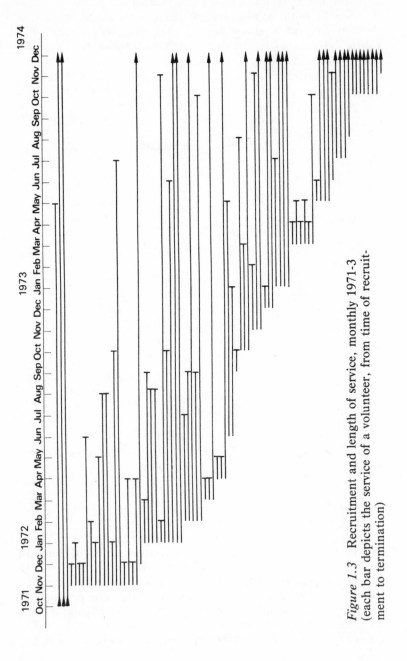

Figure 1.3 Recruitment and length of service, monthly 1971-3 (each bar depicts the service of a volunteer, from time of recruitment to termination)

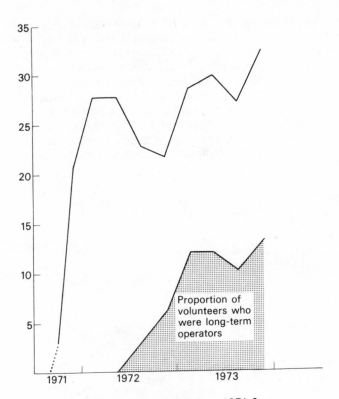

Proportion of
volunteers who
were long-term
operators

Figure 1.4 Mean list-size in each quarter, 1971-3

recruited during the first winter. Figure 1.5 demonstrates vividly the
seasonal pattern of recruitment (excluding November 1971—the
first month of the Project—which was abnormal).

On average, thirty-one new workers were recruited in each of the
two complete calendar years under review, and this level of recruitment seemed to be necessary to maintain a list of thirty-plus. But
seasonal factors meant that recruitment peaked each year in
December and January and was negligible in June and July.
Moreover, as the shaded portion in Figure 1.5 indicates, the months
when recruitment was at its peak were also the months which
produced the highest proportion of long-term volunteers (i.e. those
who served for twelve months or more): of those volunteers recruited
in mid-winter, over half became long-term operators, whereas
recruits beginning in the summer period were much less likely to
remain in service for twelve months or more.

There was no evidence that the Project organiser chose to work

The Project

differently during the summer, although she quickly sensed the variations in response, and acted accordingly. The schools were, of course, closed for six weeks in July to September, but there is no evidence to suggest that winter recruits lost interest during the summer period. It can only be concluded that a combination of factors, probably to do with the motivation of potential volunteers, leads to there being a natural tendency for recruitment to be easier in the winter, and it would appear to be wiser to work with this trend rather than against it. There would therefore seem to be every reason to concentrate recruitment campaigns during the period October to March.

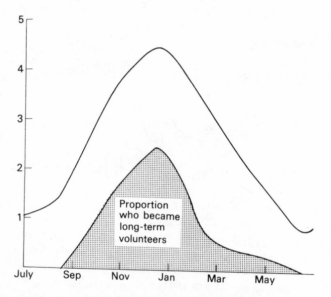

Figure 1.5 Average number of new recruits per month, 1971-3 (excluding volunteers recruited in November 1971)

Reference has already been made to the *long-term volunteers,* and there will be more about length of service in chapter 2. Of the eighty-one volunteers recruited to the Project up to January 1974, including three in post at October 1971:

28 (35 per cent) applied to the Project, but never operated;
23 (28 per cent) entered, operated and terminated their service;
30 (37 per cent) entered and were still operating at 1 January 1974.
There were none awaiting allocation.

One-fifth of the volunteers were men, and they were not disproportionately represented in any of the above groups. The nonoperators will be the subject of discussion in chapter 2. But the fifty-three operators are further distinguished into two groups:

(a) *Short-term volunteers* (N = 32) who served for one year or less up to January 1974. These are described in chapter 2;
(b) *Long-term volunteers* (N = 21) who stayed in the project for longer than twelve months. Their work is also discussed in chapter 2.

Chapter two

Operations

Non-operators

Thirty-five per cent of formal applicants to the Support Project during 1971-3 never operated. (There were others who expressed interest or made tentative inquiries, but who did not pursue the matter further.) This figure is similar to that quoted in Sparks's (1973) Merseyside study. Generally speaking, an excessively rigorous selection policy was not employed; straight rejection was used sparingly—in seven out of the eighty-one cases (9 per cent).

In four of these cases there were severe personality problems, which indicated the applicants' unsuitability, either under any circumstances, or without a degree of close supervision which the Project was not able to provide. In one case, the organiser—in the early stages of the Project—took Mrs T to meet a headmaster; throughout the interview, Mrs T appeared to be under the influence of drugs; she displayed bizarre behaviour, and the organiser had to take her out to wait in the car, while she returned to apologise to the headmaster. In another case, rejection followed the receipt of a reference which said that Mr Y had been on probation and was known to be violent and hot-tempered.

A fifth rejection involved a woman applicant who had a child at one of the schools involved in the Project, and the headmaster indicated that he thought she was quite unsuitable for the work: 'She can't look after her own child, let alone other people's.'

One girl was thought to be too young at sixteen for the kind of work involved, and she was referred to another volunteer project.

In the seventh rejection, the organiser felt 'intuitively' that the applicant should be turned down; it was a border-line decision, which was facilitated because the applicant appeared to 'put obstacles in the way' of contacting a family. 'She wasn't prepared to travel.'

A further twenty-one applicants (26 per cent) withdrew of their own volition without actually making contact with a family. They ranged from some who, had they not withdrawn, would probably have been rejected, to others who were thought by the organiser to be extremely good potential volunteers. In most cases, however, the indications were that the act of withdrawal contained a strong element of self-rejection; in twelve such cases, the reasons given by volunteers for not pursuing their application revolved around the idea that, having seen something of the Project's work, they felt that they were unsuitable or that they would not be able to spare sufficient time to undertake it. This group did not, in general create problems for the Project (although, as with all the non-operators, they collectively accounted for a sizeable portion of the organiser's time); there were difficulties, however, in three cases (including two students on a self-arranged placement) where arrangements had been made for them to meet families but in which the prospective volunteers failed to turn up.

Four withdrawals were caused by ill-health or pregnancy. In five other cases, the Project lost volunteers with whom the organiser had been impressed: in one case, the geographical location of the applicant, and the fact that she had no car, ruled her out; but in the four others, it was felt that the Project itself had precipitated withdrawal. One married couple was introduced to a headmaster but never allocated to a family; while another volunteer simply grew tired of waiting and was recruited by the probation service as a voluntary associate.

The selection of volunteers presents considerable difficulties. On the one hand, the principle underlying a scheme like the Support Project is that there is an untapped supply of men and women who are *willing* to offer help to selected children and their families said to be in need of it, and that therefore the main aim is to identify them, and, having identified them to allocate them. On the other hand, willingness is not all: *ability* is also important. The Project organiser has to bear in mind the impact that volunteers will have on the headmasters and teachers, on the children and their families, and perhaps on the other social agencies with whom the volunteers appear destined to come into contact; and to further complicate the issue, the requirements for these different parties are not necessarily identical. The headmasters and teachers will need to be assured of the sense of responsibility, the reliability and general competence of the volunteer: the Project and its organisers are, in many respects, acting as the agents of the schools and the Education Authority (indeed many of the volunteers emphasise their link with the school when families ask them to explain their role), and it is inevitable that the organiser must reflect, to some extent, the schools' view of what

17

is a suitable volunteer—hence her embarrassment when she took along a totally unsuitable person very early on in the project. Only if the organiser succeeds in securing this respect will the schools come to trust her judgment, and accept, as they did, virtually all the volunteers appointed to the Project.

As well as being acceptable to the headmasters, however, the volunteers have to be judged capable of making a relationship with and thereby *supporting* a teenage child and his or her family—or at least some parts of it. It seems probable that this ability is put to the test as soon as the first contact is established; and failure in the test may explain the relatively high drop-out rate in the first year. Volunteers who were superficially acceptable to the Project and to the headmasters may have proven unacceptable to the children or to their families.

Finally, and even more complex, there is the question of the volunteer's capacity to relate to social workers and other agencies. This may not be a question of his acceptability to them because it has been found that at least some of the advocacy style work of the volunteers involves them in real or potential conflict with hospitals, courts, Supplementary Benefits offices, social workers, housing departments, and so on.

Clearly the twin pitfalls of selection are either to exercise no control at all, thereby abdicating the manifest responsibility that the Project carries by virtue of the access that it grants to the private lives of children and their families, or to exercise so much control that the organiser finds herself appointing only those who are would-be social workers in search of a quasi-profession.

In fact the organiser's tactic of speedy rejection only in the most clear-cut cases, followed by a lengthy period during which the applicant was introduced to the work and only slowly allowed to become involved in the work of the volunteers, seemed to work well.

Short-term volunteers

One of the headmasters involved in the Project's work argued strongly that there was a real need for the provision of short-term support to families involved in crisis situations; for example, he would like to have been able to call on a volunteer to assist a family if the mother had to go into hospital for a time; and the original idea of organising the Project so that it could provide support and guidance for school-leavers as they entered the adult world also carried connotations of the short-term nature of the task. This model of operation is represented in Figure 2.1.

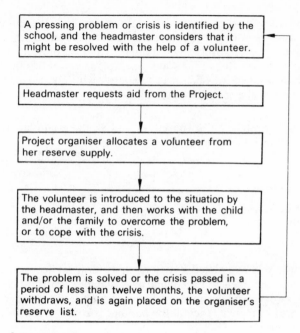

Figure 2.1

The model is close to that used traditionally by local authorities in respect of short-term fostering, and it has a number of attractions, not least the fact that it postulates a clearly definable task for the volunteers. That it failed to materialise in practice is however a lesson of prime importance both for the effective utilisation of volunteers and for the design of social work objectives overall.

The short-term volunteers (those in the Project for less than twelve months) were thirty-two in all.

Table 2.1 Short-term volunteers

Time in the Project	Service terminated	Still serving at January 1974
Up to 4 months	2	8
4 to 8 months	8	4
8 to 12 months	7	3
Total	17	15

Of those whose work was complete, a disappointingly low number of short-term volunteers were assessed by the organiser as having performed to a relatively high standard, and of those none were marked at the very top of the scale. The seriousness of this figure can be seen in perspective when it is compared with equivalent figures for the rest of the serving population.

Table 2.2 Proportion of volunteers said by the organiser to have performed to a high standard

	Service terminated %	Still serving %
Short-term volunteers	29	92
Long-term volunteers	83	100

Those who had completed a spell of short-term service were clearly the group least likely to have made a satisfactory contribution to the Project's work. And the impression is confirmed when the organiser's assessment of their impact on the families is compared with that of other workers:

Table 2.3 Proportion of volunteers said by the organiser to have had a major impact on the family

	Service terminated %	Still serving %
Short-term volunteers	6	29
Long-term volunteers	67	57

Do these disappointing results for the short-term volunteers cast doubt on their ability to fulfil the role cast for them by the operational model earlier outlined? Is the model itself inappropriate? A preliminary assessment of the evidence suggests that both these questions must be answered in the affirmative.

If we try to discover what made these people short- rather than long-term volunteers, we find that we must look for the cause, not to the client-children or families (as the operational model would suggest) but to the volunteers themselves. In fact, on a closer investigation it becomes apparent that most of these workers hardly got off the ground. For them, the whole concept of *short-term operation* with a strongly positive connotation (crisis-work, effective intervention, etc.) is quite inappropriate; most were in fact delayed non-operators. Some, like Mrs Q, started work successfully but found that, without a car, the journeys involved rendered the task quite impossible; a large proportion seemed to use the Project as a stepping-stone to other spheres—professional social work or other voluntary agencies—and stayed only long enough to discover that the Project was not sufficiently mainstream for their liking or to obtain references from the organiser; others appeared to have come looking for an interventionist task on the lines of the short-term model outlined, but then found that the work allocated to them required qualities of patience and understanding they could not summon up; another was overcome with the immensity of the job given her by the headmaster and by the sheer complexity of the family's problems; on the other hand, one visited a family for a number of months, and withdrew because she claimed there were no problems and she could find no clearly defined role to fulfil; and finally there were two who found that they were not able to condone what seemed to them to be the immoral behaviour of the family to which they had been allocated. Some of these volunteers were of a quality likely to have been able to make a significant contribution to the Project had they stayed in post, but most emerged as being unsuitable for one reason or another.

Case example   Mrs F had originally applied to the Social Services Department to work as a volunteer with them, but she said that 'they'd messed her about', and she hoped for better things from the Support Project. She was introduced to a family in which the husband had recently died; she visited the home only once, during which time she discovered that the wife had been going out with another man. She was critical of her behaviour, and was unable to offer support in such a situation. She had come into the Project expecting that she would be able to do something more active; just to go and befriend a family in need was not enough.

Moreover, the short-term model itself appeared to be of dubious validity. If the work of the volunteers was highly specific (as it sometimes is in other settings, for example, where the probation service uses voluntary associates to convey wives to visit their husbands in custody) then such a model might be appropriate. But the underlying goal of the Support Project was dependent upon the establishment of a personal relationship between the volunteer and a child or his family, and the short-term model clearly undervalued this prerequisite. The relationship that the volunteer had to offer required a considerable period of time to reach maturity.

It is not uncommon in social work, or in education, to want to achieve measurable results in a short span of time, but it is rarely possible to achieve this ambition, and it is one of the high merits of the Project that many of the volunteers were able to accept their own limitations and to work within them; but such acceptance required qualities not all volunteers possessed.

It may well be that there is indeed a need for short-term help in some situations observed by the headmasters, and local authority schemes for short-stay fostering and home helps are intended to go some way to meet this need. There is almost certainly scope for extending such provisions, but it has to be said that the Support Project did not function in such a way that it could make a significant contribution. Even though the referral may have been precipitated by a crisis, almost all the children and families referred to the organiser by the headmasters presented complex and long-standing personal and social problems; a majority of them were one-parent families, and the role of the volunteer in such cases tended to be that of a substitute parent. Both the nature of the situation and the expectations of the child were such that the quality of support was dependent upon a long-term commitment on the part of the volunteer.

Even in the one or two cases where a referral was made explicitly because of school-leaving problems, it was apparent that the volunteer could be of little help at that stage; he was coming new to an often confused situation, he had limited experience, no material resources and no direct access to other agencies. The one asset that the volunteer could bring to the relationship, and that was observed time and again in the Support Project, was his ability to use superior verbal skills, self-confidence and persistence in the face of disappointment; but even this asset could not be employed out of the context of a personal relationship. The volunteer had to be persuaded that the client and his situation were worth the effort, and the client, similarly, had to be convinced that the volunteer could be trusted. If a short-term volunteer is merely allocated to a child at the time he leaves school, there is a real risk that the child will not only have to adapt to the new working situation, but that he will also have to learn to cope with the intrusive concern of a strange outsider.

Many volunteers came to the Project with a naive conception of the problems facing the families of special school children. Some were able to change their perception of the situation, and they became the Project's long-term workers; others, looking only for a specific task, were helpfully referred to other projects (like the Council's Literacy Project, for example), where the work, though arduous, was none the less seen as being geared to a definable goal. It seems others had to begin work on the Project, in order to learn that the clients' problems were more intractable than they could tolerate, and their personal qualities did not enable them to work with the stresses and strains some children are brought up on. At that point they withdrew. Hence, it is argued, the real model for short-term operations (under twelve months) differs considerably from that outlined on page 19.

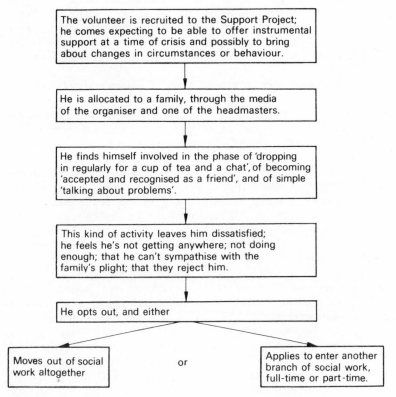

Figure 2.2   Model depicting typical short-term volunteer

Figure 2.2 depicting the typical short-term volunteer is valuable for two reasons.

(a) It reiterates that whatever the intentions of some of the school headmasters, the cases referred do not appear to have lent themselves to short-term support; if they had, the volunteers would have been able to undertake such work, and then remain with the Project by asking for further referrals. It is not possible to dismiss the earlier model altogether as being erroneous, for it may be that the Project was not properly geared to such a procedure; much of the advertising, for example, emphasised the longer-term befriending role of the volunteer. But the model must now be regarded with some scepticism because (1) the headmasters themselves tended to refer cases of extreme complexity, on the perfectly sound grounds that these were the families in greatest need; and (2) the volunteers could only respond to the problems that faced them if they patiently built up a working relationship over a lengthy period, within the context of which they could then offer help, guidance and support, and even a degree of control.

(b) It demonstrates a general point of immense significance for the development of voluntary work. Whereas the original model emphasised the organisational structure within which the volunteer would be working, the second model emphasises the equal force of the volunteer's own motivations and interests. When the scheme was launched in October 1971, an agreed pattern of working was established in which the organiser would match families to suitable volunteers; the volunteer would be interviewed by the headmaster; there would be monthly report meetings; and written records kept. All of these lent emphasis to the notion that the volunteer would be a relatively low-status member of the hierarchical structure of the school, and so indeed he remained in formal terms. But there is little doubt that the very fact of his voluntary commitment, the absence of any remuneration or even, in most cases, of adequate expenses to cover costs of different kinds, introduced a different element into a situation where power and authority are traditionally determined by professional qualifications and by how much is earned. Of course the fact that the volunteer is totally untrained and earns less than anybody else in the system is still a superficial indication of low power; but, perhaps because of this, the relationship between volunteer and family developed an independent character of its own. Once the link-up was made, the course it followed was the responsibility of the participants, and it was they who decided how it might develop. Moreover it was up to the volunteer to decide to opt out at any time that he felt the relationship was not fulfilling the kinds of expectations he had had of it. Hence it became important both to select volunteers with the personality to match the likely situations they would meet, and to be realistic about the objectives which the Project set for its volunteers. In the Support Project, the organiser was scrupulous in her descriptions of the tasks involved, but it was inevitable that some people would volunteer for the work without recognising the nature of the commitment they were making or its probable impact upon their own lives.

Voluntary work must be conceived as a two-way process between the volunteer and the family. Most of the abstract descriptions of it imply that volunteers are being recruited to fulfil a role which the schools, the social services and the community cannot apparently carry out themselves; that may be so, but, whereas the teacher, the probation officer and the organiser are paid for their professional services, the volunteer is entering into a variant of Titmuss's *Gift Relationship;* and, while his work may well be of especial value just because it is unremunerated, it is probable that its continuation is dependent upon the extent to which he feels he is receiving something in return—and it must be from the child and the family that repayment is made. The real reason for the failure of the short-term volunteers was almost certainly that in return for their efforts they did not receive the kind or degree of satisfaction they had anticipated.

Long-term volunteers

I think the most rewarding moments are when Mrs Taylor discusses some private matter with me as the only person she can talk to. She has been able to tell me her history and we have been able to sort out her worries. I have thoroughly enjoyed my work with the Taylor family and have felt really needed and welcomed in the family.

Here, in this account of a seventeen-months long relationship between a volunteer and her family, there is none of the caution, none of the professional detachment and nothing of the language that one would normally expect to find in social work literature. The volunteer was *rewarded*, she was flattered to be made privy to Mrs Taylor's problems, she felt *needed* and *welcomed*, and she thoroughly enjoyed her work. It is unrealistic not to recognise this kind of motivation among volunteers, whatever attacks may be made upon them for their Lady Bountiful image. Voluntary work must depend, like adoption, on the bringing together of two elements: A wants B, and B wants A. If the emphasis is on one half of the relationship only —A wants B but B does not want A—it seems improbable that the relationship will persist or develop to maturity.

Of the eighty-one volunteers recruited to the Project between September 1971 and January 1974, twenty-one had, by the end of the period under review, served for twelve months or more:

Table 2.4   Time served by the long-term volunteers

Time served	Service terminated	Still serving
12-17 months	2	7
18-23 months	3	3
2 years and over	1	5
Total long-term volunteers	6	15

Many of those still operating were committed to remaining in contact as long as they felt they were needed, or until personal circumstances compelled them to withdraw. Of the six who had terminated service already: two did so because of removal from the district, one because he found his relationship with the boy impossible to sustain and three withdrew partly because they felt they were not needed any more and partly because of difficulties over transport, time or other commitments.

The success or failure of the Project depended on the work of its long-term operators. The process of recruitment, selection, induction, and the building of a relationship between worker and family would have been largely worthless unless it had led to the accumulation of a core of committed volunteers working on a long-term basis with families and children in need of support. It is evident that, by that test, the Support Project achieved much in its initial phase of operation: to have secured the long-term services of one-quarter of all those who volunteered for the Project is a worthy result.

Table 2.5   Performance and impact achieved by long-term volunteers

	Service terminated %	Still serving %
Proportion of volunteers said by the organiser to have performed to a high standard	83	100
Proportion of volunteers said by the organiser to have had a major impact on the family	67	57

The importance of the long-term volunteers is confirmed by the organiser's assessments of their performance and impact. Every current long-term volunteer was said to be performing to a high standard; all except one from the past were similarly assessed. There is almost certainly a complex interaction here, involving the links between volunteers, families and the Project organiser. The performance mark is an assessment of the smooth working of the arrangement, of the quality of the relationship between volunteer and family, of the suitability of the volunteer for the nature of the work available in the Project, and of the realistic attitude of the volunteer towards his role *vis-à-vis* the family. Relationships with the schools and the headmasters were also good in most of these cases.

Reference has already been made to Nokes's useful distinction between the twin roles of the social worker: that in which a virtuoso performance is given and the general care role. Nokes has argued that the tendency among professionals is towards a greater emphasis on the virtuoso performance of using skilled intervention with a view to achieving measurable results. He has suggested that there are strong social pressures to support such a trend because of the higher status that goes with it (the work of the surgeon, compared with that of the nurse). But, as Nokes has also suggested, it is probable that the scope for the virtuoso performer is extremely limited, and the state of current knowledge in social work is such that the value of virtuoso skills is much less than is sometimes believed; on the other hand there is little doubt that the need for the general care role is growing rather than diminishing, with the breakdown in neighbourhood communities, the increasing number of old people, the emphasis on community care for the mentally/physically sick and handicapped, and the accumulating complexity of social organisation in an urban setting. And certainly it was a form of general care that the volunteers in the Support Project were called upon to practise. It would be wrong to suggest that they provided intensive, ongoing care on anything like the scale that is possible in residential settings; but, given the limitation of working in the community, the long-term volunteers were certainly involved with their families to a very close degree. In practising a form of social advocacy, the volunteers were meeting some hitherto unmet needs for caring; and, by using their personal resources of self-confidence and social maturity, time and energy, they were able to provide support for a selection of teenage children and their families, and to help them handle and overcome some of the everyday problems that confronted them.

Bearing this in mind, the concept of *impact* must be interpreted appropriately. It was not anticipated that the volunteers would change the behaviour of the children to whom they were allocated but that they would play an active role in helping, guiding, supporting and caring for the child and/or other members of his family. The organiser, using fairly strict criteria, felt that these hopes had been fulfilled by between one-half and two-thirds of the long-term volunteers.

Figure 2.3 applying to these volunteers differs from that outlined for the short-term operators.

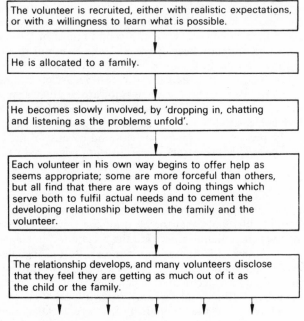

Figure 2.3 The long-term process

There was, of course, no set pattern. In some cases, the volunteer worked closely with the child, and found the adult members of the family unattractive; in others, the volunteer was increasingly drawn into work with the mother or father; sometimes there was maximum effort spent on practical activities; in other situations the volunteer continued visiting until needs he felt able to respond to arose.

The Project provided an additional community resource through the medium of its long-term volunteers. In the process of accumulating the team, a great deal of effort went into the organisational task, but this had to be weighed against the fact that for thirty families at a time a form of social supervision and aid was being made available which would otherwise not have been there, and that for fifteen of these the support was on a long-term basis.

It is clear to those who observed the Project from its inception that the practical benefits obtained by many of the families supported fully justified the time and money spent in its establishment.

Role of the organiser

The Support Project arose out of the need, felt within two or three special schools, for the provision of social work support for the families of children at risk or for the children themselves. Although two of the schools shared a teacher-counsellor and other schools had nominated teachers for home-school liaison it was apparent that such appointments were insufficient to provide ongoing intensive help of the kind thought necessary, and there was no immediate prospect of any full-time social work appointments in the schools even if that were thought to be an appropriate step to take. Accordingly it was decided to try and tap the resources of the community and to secure the active involvement of volunteers. However it was quickly discovered that to maintain an adequate supply of recruits would itself involve a degree of time and effort not available from within the existing resources of the schools or voluntary organisations. Hence, funds were sought from the DHSS to appoint an organiser. In this way, the organiser's role was delineated from the outset: she would be responsible for recruiting and allocating suitable volunteers so that they might be put in touch with appropriate children and families by the schools. The implication was that the primary working relationship, once established, would be a triangular one, involving the volunteer, the school, and the family and/or child. (See Figure 2.4.)

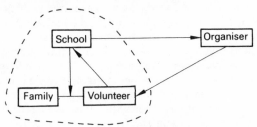

Figure 2.4

In such a model, the organiser would undertake the introductory work on the school's behalf, and then withdraw to leave the school to supervise and control its additional volunteer-resources.

Operations

In practice the work of the Project deviated significantly from this model, with the organiser playing a more active role *vis-à-vis* the volunteers in post. (See Figure 2.5.)

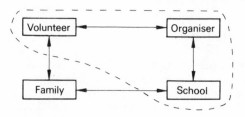

Figure 2.5

As planned, the organiser exercised full responsibility for advertising, recruitment, vetting applicants and organising introductory meetings: but in addition to allocating volunteers to schools for matching with families by the headmasters, she was very much more deeply involved with the ongoing provision of support. In particular she was able to establish close working relationships with four or five of the headmasters, and, significantly, they were the ones who made the most active use of the Project's volunteers; they came to rely on her discretion and judgment, and it is arguable that, had this not been the case, the trouble of accepting full responsibility for supervising the volunteers would have been great enough to deter the headmasters from using the scheme.

One of the strongest features of the Project was the close relationship that developed between the organiser and each of the volunteers. Once a volunteer was allocated to a school, the organiser did not disclaim all further responsibility; she maintained brief records about the volunteer's work, encouraged them to keep in touch with her by phone or letter and, if she had not heard from any for a month or so, took the initiative in making contact. In addition, she organised regular meetings at which lectures were given; these meetings were reasonably well attended. She invited volunteers to her own home. Every term a review meeting was held in each school at which volunteers reported on the progress of their respective families, exchanged information with the headmasters and teachers, sought guidance from them and from a representative of the Social Services Department, and discussed future plans. At times these could be critical occasions: whether or not a child should be removed to a residential school (the decision was made, of course, by the Education Department, but the volunteer's description of his experiences in the child's home helped to fill out the picture), whether a volunteer could continue to work with a child whose company he could not bear, how to establish adequate liaison with the social worker or probation officer involved, whether a child was suffering from malnutrition and so on. In all these ways, the organiser shared with the volunteers their problems and concerns; it was stated at the outset of the Project that the person to be appointed to the organiser's post should be 'an administrator rather than a social worker'. That distinction remained valid, but the administration extended beyond the necessary task of recruiting volunteers to that of supervising them when in post. Hence, it is necessary to emphasise the continuing interaction that occurred between the organiser and the headmasters, and the organiser and the volunteers, with all three parties coming together in the once-a-term meetings at the schools. This model also reflects the point, made earlier, that while the school might have had a link with the family through the child, it was apparent that many of the long-term volunteers developed a much closer relationship with the family itself, and that after the initial period, this tended to assume proportions which made it relatively independent of the school.

Part two

Volunteers and clients

Chapter three

Volunteers and the schools

In chapters 4 to 6 a detailed, qualitative analysis of the part played by thirty-three volunteers in the Support Project is attempted. They represent not a sample but the total population of volunteers who, by mid-summer 1974, had completed twelve months in the Project (N = 28), plus five active volunteers who were identified by the organiser as being well-established in their work and likely to become long-term operators. The methodological disadvantages of using data from a relatively small population are well known; suffice it to say that whatever its shortcomings, the present study represents a rare attempt to balance the opinions and attitudes of both the givers and recipients of a social work service, and that the limited range of the study does not in any way reduce its validity or its relevance to the discussion of voluntary service; doubt arises only over the extent to which it may be regarded as reliably representative of voluntary work as a whole. The study is about one project with special features, but the information about that project—which, as we argued in chapters 1 and 2, had an unusually effective organiser —directs our attention to questions which have implications for the development of volunteer programmes as a whole, and indeed for the organisation of support services generally.

The volunteers were characteristic of other projects, so far as their age and sex were concerned. (Table 3.1.)

Almost all the volunteers came to the Project in response to a variety of advertising procedures employed by the MCVS and the Project organiser; and they all passed through a process of absorption into the Project, including interviews with the organiser, the provision of references, introduction to the school and its headmaster, and introduction to the child or family chosen for support.

Table 3.1 Age and sex of the volunteers

age	male	female	total
20s	1	8	9
30s	1	7	8
40s	3	5	8
50s	—	5	5
60s	—	3	3
Total	5	28	33

School settings

Six of Manchester's special schools were most actively involved in the scheme over the three-year period, but the attitudes of the respective headmasters varied from total commitment, through muted enthusiasm, to scepticism and a feeling that the limited pay-off from the scheme gave it only low priority in the headmaster's strategic plans. The Project had been conceived as a way of meeting the schools' need to provide a counselling and support service to selected children and their families. The most consistent support for it came from the two headmasters who seemed to accord highest priority to this end and who had been able to make the most effective arrangements for home-school liaison responsibilities to be carried by a member of staff. The two headmasters who had made the least use of the scheme both said that if they were able to appoint specialist home-school liaison teachers in the future, then they would envisage a change of heart, for that would enable the volunteers to be more adequately supervised within the school structure. Those who employed volunteers most effectively were certainly the headmasters who offered the most direct access and who gave the most clear-cut and direct supervision; this did not undermine the essential autonomy of the volunteer-client relationship, and it provided a framework within which the volunteer could operate. These headmasters and their liaison teachers felt that the volunteers should be given some preparation for the task, and that their objectives should be limited though long-term; they thought that the school should be responsible for bringing together the two parties and that the nature of the relationship should be made explicit from the start. Significantly both these headmasters were members of the Project's advisory group, both remained committed to its explicit objective of providing support, and both were opposed to any major changes in direction. They differed, however, in the forcefulness of their approach. One was much more authoritarian and managerial than the other; he said that unless he was allowed to retain total control over the work of the volunteers he would want nothing to do with the scheme. Hence, in its most positive manifestations, the Project provided additional staff for use within the traditional school structure as it moved tentatively out into the families of the children; both headmasters placed a high priority on the school's social work responsibilities and were highly critical of the failure of professional social workers to function effectively in this respect.

At the other extreme were two headmasters who, in interview, expressed regret and some disappointment at having failed to make more successful use of the scheme. Neither of them were negative men; both were energetic and impressive in furthering the welfare of their schools and its children. But their attitudes towards the volunteers and their experiences with them reflected the fact that they were not convinced of its value in their situation.

Mr Wilkins is regarded as a man who would lay more emphasis on the value of formal education (in the three 'Rs' sense) than some of his colleagues, and in interview he expressed disappointment about the Project in practice. He said he had found difficulty in identifying suitable families for the volunteers: either they had no problems, or their problems were too numerous and complex. With regard to one particularly difficult boy, he felt that since the volunteers stopped their involvement, 'he is no worse, and may even be better'. He offered no close supervision, but felt that the position would be very different if he were able to appoint a special teacher to take responsibility for the scheme; in any case, however, he had become sceptical about the vague nature of the support task, and thought that volunteers might be better employed in more clearly defined roles—for example, undertaking a form of after-care with school-leavers, or going away with small parties of children and helping to provide supervision in the school's outdoor pursuits centre.

Mr Behrens has a firm commitment to getting his school accepted as a useful and integral part of the local community, and to this end he makes extensive use of parents and other voluntary helpers from the immediate vicinity of the school; the Project's volunteers did not fit into this scheme because they tended to come from areas of the city far distant from the school. In order to combat the school's image as the 'Daft School', from which he feels his children suffer acutely, the headmaster organises youth clubs and has built an adventure playground; Mr Behrens is emphatically not opposed to the use of volunteers, but the Project's recruits did not conform to his community development profile.

Mr Behrens feels he has not had much benefit from the four volunteers allocated to him. He had hoped for self-assured activists who would relate easily to the children, but found that most of them conformed to the traditional Lady Bountiful image. As a result, he allocated them to children and families who 'could use a bit of charity'. He was unable to give any supervision; if he had done so, he felt that he might as well have been seeing the families himself—it was no saving. He too felt, like Mr Wilkins, that the impending appointment of a specialist home-school liaison teacher might make all the difference in that such a person might see it as his prime responsibility to organise the volunteers effectively; furthermore, Mr Behrens would prefer to use the volunteers for much more specific purposes; helping at camp, providing transport, running youth club nights, helping in the school and at special school events.

In comparing the headmasters, there are significant differences in their relationships with the Project. Some are committed to the aims of the Project, and see the provision of case-work support in the home as a prime responsibility of the school if the school is to function adequately as a special educational institution; they viewed the recruitment of volunteers as a legitimate means of achieving that end. Hence they related well to the Project organiser; they tended to be sympathetic towards hesitant, inexperienced or inferior volunteers (for example, using them in cautious ways before introducing them to a family). Since they had limited expectations of social intervention in general and of the volunteers in particular, they provided more or less close supervision, and maintained a close interest in the developing relationship between volunteer and client. The fact that they offered effective support to the volunteers does not mean that they were necessarily better headmasters than those who were less supportive. Both Mr Behrens and Mr Wilkins were conscientious and able headmasters, but they were less committed to the aims of the Project, and the volunteers attached to their schools found that their performance was adversely affected by the less than whole-hearted support they received. To that extent, the volunteer is very much a part of the social system into which he is recruited, and, although his work with the client can assume independent proportions, his initial staying-power and satisfaction may be affected by the permanent employees whom he meets.

Chapter four

What the volunteers did

Whatever the intention of the Project initiators, the focus of the volunteers' work varied considerably.

Table 4.1 Focus of the volunteers' work

	N	%
Family as a whole	9	28
Mother and child	5	16
Mother alone	8	25
Child alone	10	31
Total	32	100
No information	1	
Total	33	

Thus, in the majority of cases (69 per cent) the family, either in whole or in part, was the focus of the volunteer's efforts. To that extent, the workers confirmed the view reflected in chapter 2 that the Project became committed more to family counselling than to getting a school-leaver into work.

The volunteers were asked to describe in considerable detail the kinds of activities they pursued with their clients. Table 4.2 indicates the number of volunteers who mentioned every type of activity at least once; of course, the table gives no indication of the weight that any volunteer gave to any one type.

It is possible to compare this analysis with a number of similar

Table 4.2 The activities of the volunteers

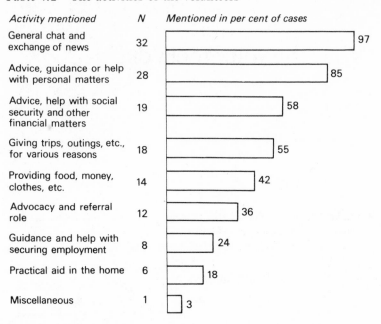

Activity mentioned	N	Mentioned in per cent of cases
General chat and exchange of news	32	97
Advice, guidance or help with personal matters	28	85
Advice, help with social security and other financial matters	19	58
Giving trips, outings, etc., for various reasons	18	55
Providing food, money, clothes, etc.	14	42
Advocacy and referral role	12	36
Guidance and help with securing employment	8	24
Practical aid in the home	6	18
Miscellaneous	1	3

studies made of professional case-work practice, and to reach a conclusion about the nature of the work undertaken by most of the volunteers. The volunteers placed greater emphasis on practical activities than has been the tradition among case-workers, but in the majority of cases, such a practical focus was none the less restricted, and on a number of occasions, its value and effectiveness were open to doubt. As with full-time social workers, the volunteers found that their major task and the most feasible tactic was to concentrate on verbal exchange and on offering guidance, advice or help with regard to a variety of personal or practical problems.

Practical aid in the home

Even the figure of 18 per cent is deceptively high in this area of activity, for it was found either that the practical help was often slight or there was a discrepancy between the volunteer's account and that of the family. In two cases, volunteers had helped with dressmaking and hairdressing but in the others where claims were made that the volunteers had undertaken cleaning or decorating tasks, there was some evident discomfiture or ambivalence on the part of the families (and in one case, the headmaster) as to whether this was an appropriate role for the volunteer. It seemed to involve an unsolicited and unwelcomed intrusion into affairs that were thought to be none of the volunteer's business and it risked overstepping the sensitive boundary which marked out the family's independence. Maybe there would be cases where this might not be so, but it is significant that, in general, the volunteers appear to have decided that either such behaviour would not be appropriate to their role and status or it would not be acceptable to the recipient.

This is an important conclusion, because a large number of recruits to the Project began with the idea that such practical involvement was the sort of activity beckoning them; this is often mentioned with regard to the idea of voluntary work with the elderly. But, as we shall see in other respects, it is important for most families to restrict the amount of practical giving or to ensure that they too give in return. Free charring is all right when it is done by a state-paid home help (if you can get one) but it is not an appropriate activity for an unpaid outsider who has been introduced to you as variously a 'volunteer', 'a friend of the headmaster', or just 'someone who will help'. Help, maybe; but not interference.

Guidance and help with securing work

The fact that in only eight cases did the volunteer offer practical or verbal assistance in securing work is a measure of the Project's failure to fulfil one of its original aims: that of helping the school-leaver obtain work and settle into his adult role. Indeed, the figure is even then exaggerated, because in two cases the help was given not to the child but to a parent, and in two others the reference indicates the volunteer's role was superficial in the extreme; there is only one recorded instance of a volunteer successfully steering a child into a job which he might not have obtained otherwise.

In general, then, the volunteers did not function in the employment sector, partly because the majority of clients had not yet left school, and partly because either they or the children did not see it as appropriate or feasible behaviour in the circumstances. It was apparent that some volunteers were hesitant to play an active role, and felt they had little to offer that was not already available through the Careers Office or the school; where others attempted to take active steps to encourage a client to get a job or change his employment for something better, the overtures were mostly rejected.

Advocacy and the referral role

The impression had been gained in interviews with the Project organiser that the advocacy role best characterised the work being undertaken by the majority of the volunteers, and that it was a source of mutual satisfaction to the volunteer and the family. In theory, the usually superior verbal skills of the volunteer could be put to good use on behalf of clients unaccustomed to finding their way through the labyrinth of the social services. The reality was somewhat different; the advocacy/referral role applied in about one-third (36 per cent) of the cases, and although in some instances there was indeed mutual satisfaction (as where the volunteer had helped secure improved accommodation), in the majority of cases there seemed to be elements of frustration and resentment. This tended to emerge with either the client being disappointed at the volunteer's failure to get results (as a result of which the volunteer was occasionally compared critically with professional social workers) or with the volunteer concluding with some bitterness that he had come to feel that he was 'being used by' the family.

Agencies involved in this aspect of the volunteer's work included the Family Planning Association ('I'd like to get her on the pill—she don't want no more'), psychiatric and hospital clinics, the Social Services Department (over the question of restrainers for a severely subnormal child), the Housing Department, and the Supplementary Benefits Commission. (When Mrs Foster went along to the SBC, she was firmly advised that she was misguided in trying to act on behalf of her family—'they're just using you'.)

One or two of the volunteers, particularly forceful characters, were able to seek to influence both the family itself and the agencies around it to a remarkable extent. One such person seemed to break every single rule about self-determination in social work, and much to the amused admiration of the headmaster and the Social Services Department representative, she set about getting the family organised with gusto. But, for the most part, the volunteers did not know their way around the system any better than the clients; many of them were even more nervous or hesitant than some of the families; and they did not have the benefit of having either informal contacts or a professional base with which to exert the kind of influence that social workers may do. It is significant that one of the most successful of the advocates was the wife of a Labour councillor, who drew on her husband's contacts to benefit the family. Social advocacy and acting as a referral agency are skilled techniques which the majority of the volunteers did not have at the outset; that some might develop them is not the point. The assumption underlying the project was that they would bring such skills with them and, generally speaking, that was not found to be the case.

Providing food, money, clothes, etc.

Every Christmas, the evening papers are full of news stories and photographs recording the persistence of charity in its most traditional form: food parcels for the elderly, toys for poor children, presents for the disadvantaged. And through the year, organisations like the Women's Royal Voluntary Service and the Family Service Units make good use of other peoples' cast-off clothing. Moreover, the giving of money is not only institutionalised in government departments, but persists in hundreds of odd corners with the availability of trust funds for the poor, administered both by social work agencies like the Family Welfare Association, and by specialist professional and local associations too.

So far as the volunteers were concerned, the giving of goods or cash proved to be a sensitive and sometimes embarrassing issue. At one extreme, there were a small group (about 15 per cent) who gave items over a long period of time, and felt it to be a perfectly appropriate way of fulfilling their role: 'all we can do now is to see that Edith doesn't go short of anything'. They had come to terms with the fact that they 'were being used purely for material gain'. The rest of the giving (27 per cent) was more spasmodic, and was conducted somewhat selfconsciously. Most preferred not to give money, and many were not sure whether they had been right to give anything—clothes were the usual commodity involved.

Some families were quite happy to accept gifts: referring to the clothes the volunteer brought, one said, 'that's about all she's done really'. But others were anxious not to be put into a markedly inferior position; in one case, in which there was a very easy relationship between volunteer and family, the volunteer drove the family to a residential school to visit their son, but the family insisted on paying for the petrol. Much seemed to depend on the nature of the relationship established: in those cases where it came closest to being a friendship, it was clear that the giving had to be reciprocated in some form or other; where the volunteer was seen as a quasi-social worker/official, gifts were accepted without much fuss; but in the few cases, where there was animosity in the relationship, giving could be seen as adding fuel to the fires of emotion—in one case, where the parents thought that the volunteer was corrupting their daughter, the gifts were seen as bribery with evil intent.

The volunteers' feeling of the need for caution where gifts were concerned seems justified, not so much in the light of actual evidence of difficulties that arose in specific cases, but because of the undoubted significance that acts of giving and receiving had for the volunteer, the family or both. Many volunteers referred to the dangers of making families over-dependent on them, and the need to encourage independence; unfortunately, the research provides little information to support these ideas. Certainly no family seemed to have become over-dependent as a result of the work of even the most intensively committed volunteer, and the movement towards independence was best achieved in a case where the volunteer had been generous with his time, his money, his energy and his emotional commitment. These attitudes reflect the fact that the exchange of goods could epitomise the nature of the relationship established, and that it is important for it to be appropriate in the eyes of both giver and recipient. This is much more important than asserting either that giving is in all circumstances wrong, or that it should necessarily be an element present in any voluntary helping situation. It simply reflects a specific element of inequality in the relationship, which may often be accepted without embarrassment by both parties; it need not be immutable, and it should not be synonymous with moral inequality. But the very establishment of a Support Project presupposes that some have much to give to others in need, and material aid is a perfectly legitimate element in the giving process. It is not irrelevant to note that when the clients were asked to assess the value of the help they had received from the Project, many of them answered in specifically material terms.

Giving trips, outings, etc.

The largest proportionate commitment to active help on the part of the volunteers involved journeys. The volunteers—for the most part—made use of their cars to give the children the kinds of experiences that they might give to their own children: trips to toy-shops, cinemas, swimming baths, picnics, the airport and Belle Vue zoo park. There was evidence that both children and parents had appreciated these trips, but in most cases they occurred at intermittent intervals. In some cases, the more determined volunteers undertook the responsibility on a more ambitious scale, but most of them found there were limits in the extent to which they could function at this level. In one case, a particularly difficult boy finally drove his volunteer to withdraw from the Project because he insisted on visiting the airport every week. In another case a volunteer extended his support to a crippled neighbour of the family's and gave her a car-ride to a town twelve miles away so she could visit her sister for the first time in seventeen years.

In a more controlling role one lady, in consultation with the headmaster, used her car to convey a girl to school every morning. The child had been a persistent truant, and it was thought that the problem could be best overcome by exercising this control; however, after some months, it was learnt that the pattern of truancy had remained unchanged. As soon as the volunteer had left her at the school gates, the girl had turned away and reverted to her normal behaviour—but the attempt at control led to an inherently dishonest relationship between them since the girl was forced to claim she had been to school as intended.

Overall, the giving of rides seemed to present none of the problems associated with other forms of material aid (except in the case already referred to where the parents insisted on contributing towards the cost of petrol); it was a favour which the privileged adult could bestow on the less privileged child without inducing feelings of guilt or embarrassment in the volunteer or of indebtedness or resentment on the part of the family. It was a precise role which the volunteer could play, producing a feeling of fulfilment in him and apparent enjoyment in the child. The schools encouraged this kind of commitment, and some spoke of it in somewhat grandiose educational terms as broadening restricted horizons, enlarging the child's experience, and so on; most of the volunteers preferred to think of it as giving a treat. In three of the cases listed under this heading, the events were not so much trips, as offering situations which improved the quality of the child's leisure-time: visiting the volunteer's house to draw, to make models or to sew, and, in one case, arranging for the boy to join the Boys' Brigade—a step which rendered the volunteer's own continued presence virtually redundant.

Verbal support

The primary tool available to every volunteer was his tongue. By visiting the family or arranging to meet the child, he was committed to entering into conversation, and both volunteers and families indicated that they recognised the main element in the support relationship did indeed consist of conversation. In virtually all cases, the exchange of gossip, information and comment was a central activity, while in almost as many (85 per cent), it was agreed that the volunteers had offered guidance, advice or help with personal problems in the family. Similarly, in a large proportion of cases (58 per cent), advice of a specifically financial kind had been given— often in connection with claiming Social Security benefits.

Thus, like most professional social workers in the community,

45

these volunteers were mainly engaged on the development and use of a personal relationship for the benefit of the client. They became known to their families and to the children, listened to them, discussed their difficulties, and responded as best they could—sometimes with actions, but more often with words. The words, however, could be quite forceful and controlling; hence Mr Grice responded to the headmaster's request, and set about the task of persuading Richard that going to a special residential school would be in his own best interests—he succeeded and confessed that he thought this was 'the only thing of importance I've done'. In another case, the headmaster asked a volunteer to give firm directions on contraception to a girl at school, and so help her avoid giving birth to children since they would probably be of very low IQ; the volunteer did not feel able to accept this commission and was more concerned to broaden the girls experience and help her prepare for the time when she would leave school.

There were a few instances where verbal exchanges were something of an effort: Mrs Hammerton was never asked to sit down when she visited her family and only ever stayed a few minutes; Mrs Whitehouse now visits briefly and confesses to putting up a barrier between herself and the family: the mother 'is the last person I would choose for a friend'. In cases like this, the family told us that they saw the volunteer very much in 'official' terms, with the result that conversation was necessarily stilted and potentially hostile. But in the majority of cases, this was not so; friendship of a kind tended to blossom, so that the family spoke of the ease with which they could converse: one liked the volunteer very much and 'preferred her to the probation officer who would always try to change the subject'. There was usually a slight element of awe and of gratitude, reflecting the fact that the volunteer retained the power to withdraw from the relationship if he so chose. In only a handful of cases, did it move in the direction of equality, with any member of the family coming freely to the volunteer's house, with a mother offering advice to the volunteer or with the child free to call the tune as he chose. The best example of this comes from Mrs Mackintosh, who commented that her own home conditions and financial circumstances were inferior to those of the client; Mrs Scott bought presents for the volunteer's little girl, and told us that she and the volunteer got on like a house on fire; she felt they were really equals, and she had found it easy to accept the volunteer's help.

Conclusion

There is no dominant pattern emergent from the analysis of the volunteers' activities, nor is there any clear indication that any particular approach is more likely to meet with the family's approval.

The activities undertaken were generally a reflection of the family's needs as diagnosed by the volunteer and as negotiated with one or more members of the family; but they also reflected the interests, ideas and resources of each volunteer. Hence some were more forceful than others and some found it easier to relate to one of the adult members of the family than to the child. No general directions were given to the volunteers, and specific guidance in isolated cases only; the activities developed from the bringing together of the two key elements in the Project: the volunteer and the family. There can be no typical or best pattern established: at one extreme there is Mrs Martin doing pretty well everything and incurring the half-amused criticism of onlooking social workers as she breaks every rule in the guide book to non-directive case-work; on the other, there is Mrs Surrey practising a form of quiet anonymity and achieving much more in the eyes of the boy's grandparents than her own self-denigration had led us to expect.

The only hint of a lesson to be learnt from the Project is that most of the volunteers who came under fire from their families had involved themselves in the full range of practical activities; it may be that, unless the volunteer has the forcefulness and the willpower to carry it off (like Mrs Martin), to do *too* much in the house, to give *too* many presents and to take the children out *too* frequently is to run the risk of intruding beyond the limits of privacy and independence even the most downtrodden family is prepared to allow. The best volunteers moved warily (but not hesitantly) at the outset, and sought to establish an understanding and workable relationship with their families before offering too much in the way of forceful advice or material aid; in this way, they expressed their recognition that the family was under no obligation to accept them in their midst, but that they could turn to them if need should arise. The establishment of this voluntary contract proved to be one of the hardest of all tasks for the volunteer—as indeed it is for the professional social worker—but for those who achieved it, the range of activities open was very wide indeed.

In half the cases there was clear evidence that the frequency of contacts had declined. Most of the families received visits from their volunteer at least once a fortnight for a part of the time that they were in the Project, but for the majority there was a falling-off in frequency after six months or after a specific crisis had passed. By the time we interviewed the volunteers, it was clear that in eighteen out of the thirty-three cases, visits were taking place monthly or less often; most of them claimed that the family would contact them if they needed help, but the viability of a weekly contact was no longer accepted: there was nothing to talk about, nothing to do, the *raison d'être* of the allocation was questioned, or the volunteer had lost his initial enthusiasm. Hence the whole concept of *activities* seemed in many of the cases to be linked to the initial period of contact. Finally the length of time spent on the visits varied from an average of ten minutes to an average of two to three hours. The mean time would be around one hour.

We conclude therefore that the reality is extremely variable, but that the nearest one can get to a norm would look like this: The volunteer visits her family once every week or fortnight at the outset, but gradually reduces the frequency; she usually spends about an hour there talking to the mother and/or the child; they will exchange news about their respective families, and talk more specifically about the client's current concerns; the volunteer will exercise her superior position by giving advice where it seems appropriate, and may help the mother to obtain her benefits from the Social Security office; if she has a car, she's likely to take the child out once or twice, and she may rather hesitantly offer the family some second-hand clothes which her own family have grown out of.

Inherent in this is the fact it is the volunteer who exercises the initiative in all these matters; she is the leading partner in the relationship; but she is not and cannot be a dominant partner: she is a visitor to the house (and will be unlikely to invite the clients back to her own home), and so must tread cautiously in the full realisation that anything she does has to be broadly acceptable to the family. The relationship, like all voluntary relationships, is a negotiated one. It may not be one between equals, but the clients retain strong powers of rejection and veto which they do not hesitate to use at any time. The *support* that the project has to offer can only be given if the family and/or the child is prepared to receive it—and their retention of the power to refuse help is their crucial element of independence that no volunteer, no social service agency has a right to challenge except at very great cost to the society in which we live.

Chapter five

Volunteer/client opinions

It was argued in the last chapter that within broad limits, volunteers functioned in very different ways, and that these variations reflected not only their own attitudes and interests but also the responses made by their client children and families. Some peoples' faith in the certain value of putting in a volunteer to lend support to a child or family in need presupposes the kind of simple relationship which is rarely, if ever, found in social work. Even if the task to be tackled by the volunteer was clearly defined and described, much would still depend upon the reaction of those who were presumed to be in need of help; but, when as in this project, the task is deliberately imprecise, and is rendered more so by the different degrees of commitment felt by respective headmasters responsible for the initial referral, then the untried volunteer is likely to find himself in an open-ended situation in which the family's perceptions of him will determine the outcome of his intervention at least as much as will his view of them.

In the Support Project, there were a large number of cases in which the volunteer was directly or indirectly, courteously or abruptly rejected by the family at a very early stage; such instances are not reflected in this account, however, because of its concentration on the 'successful' volunteers who lasted long enough to be expected to make some kind of significant impact on the families to whom they were allocated. But even in these select instances, the attitudes of the clients varied greatly, and although the volunteers were technically 'successful', not all would be regarded as such by the families to which they had been allocated.

How does the volunteer perceive the family?

The attitudes expressed by volunteers span the full spectrum:

Mr Jameson admires, respects and sympathises with the mother, and thinks she has fulfilled her responsibilities bravely; she reminds him very much of his own mother during his childhood. The family are eager recipients of his help and advice, and he enjoys his visits there.

Mrs Martin too sympathises with the mother, likes her, and feels that she can identify with her: 'I was a Carol once'. She thinks the father is lazy and workshy, but she has learnt to understand his attitudes. She would love to organise the family and mobilise resources for them: 'If only I could get them rehoused, then I could really get her round to my way of thinking'.

Although feeling coolly sympathetic to them in their plight, *Mrs Whitehouse* finds it impossible to put herself at ease with the family; she describes the mother as 'the last person in the world I would choose for a friend' and confesses that she puts up a barrier between herself and the family to keep them at bay. It wasn't always so, for Mrs Whitehouse used to visit together with her husband, and he played a very active part in the early days; but then the Whitehouse's marriage broke down, and she could not bring herself to tell the family why her husband no longer came to visit with her. 'It's my private life, and I don't see why I should share it with these people.'

Mr Riviere admits that he quickly developed a strong dislike for the boy to whom he had been allocated (an earlier volunteer working with the same boy claimed she liked him in 'a funny sort of way' but taking him out became a menial task and she grew to dread it, 'it depressed me'). There was nothing about him that he could take to; he sensed no appreciation of his efforts, and felt he was just being used.

Taking the group as a whole:

23 (70 per cent) said that they liked the member of the family with whom they were working (of these, most said that they liked the whole family, but 4 to 12 per cent identified one or more members whom they disliked);

8 (24 per cent) had mixed feelings about the family as a whole;

2 (6 per cent) actively disliked the client who was the main focus of their work.

Thus, although the range is wide, the distribution is distinctly biased. Over two-thirds of the volunteers were functioning in a situation where they enjoyed the company of their clients—and indeed, for the most part, felt that the word 'client' conveyed the wrong idea of the relationship as it had developed.

In two-thirds of the cases, the volunteers spoke of the hardships which the family was facing, and said that their main feeling was one of sympathy; none expressed any attitudes of condemnation, although some were explicitly right-wing in their generalised opinions about poverty and deviance in society; they tended to dissociate these opinions from the individual families to which they had been attached. In the remaining one-third, problems were not evident to anything like the same extent, and sometimes the volunteer could not see why he had been allocated to the case; in all these instances, the volunteer perceived the family as a remarkably happy unit, and found it fairly easy to work within it with a view to developing its own resources.

Families' views

We asked the member of the family who had had most to do with each volunteer how he felt about him. The answers were allocated by the interviewer to a position along a five-point scale, with the following results.

Table 5.1   Families' views of the volunteers

	N	%
Enthusiastic	2	6
Positive	13	37
Fairly positive	9	27
Passively accepting, non-committal	9	27
Hostile	1	3
Total	34	100

(The total of thirty-four interviews reflects the fact that no interview could be obtained in one family, while two family members were interviewed separately in two families.)

There was a greater volume of essentially positive comments from this population than in many parallel studies of the clients of social workers. Even within the non-committal group, there was little evidence of resentment or resistance to the volunteer's efforts; the opinions were a reflection of the failure of the relationship to survive long enough for positive feelings to emerge, and this was often as much the responsibility of the volunteer as of the client: 'She was nice, but I hardly knew her'; 'She didn't persevere long enough.' Some expressed negative feelings, but admitted they were sorry the volunteer had now stopped visiting. A small group were more strongly critical: 'She's like a social worker—seems very hard, not easy to get on with.' and 'I just get on with the job and that's it; I don't want people hanging around, and that's what she (the

volunteer) did. She was all right, but there was no need for her . . ..
They're all snoopers, if you want it straight.' In only one family did
anybody speak out with unequivocal hostility; the parents (but not
the daughter on whom the work was focused) accused the volunteer
of being useless, false and insidious and of corrupting their child by
blackmail, bribery and incitement to sexual licence; there was no
evidence of truth in the allegations and they caused the daughter
some distress.

Within the remaining group of 70 per cent who expressed positive
views about their volunteers, the closer the volunteer approximated
to a personal friend with whom the client could identify, the more
enthusiastic were the attitudes expressed. A particular illustration of
this was the way in which families always mentioned instances when
the volunteers had invited them to their own homes or had brought
their husbands, wives, children or friends to the client's home; this
action so clearly stamped the relationship with a strongly personal
quality that it merited especial mention and almost always improved
the image of the volunteer in the eyes of his clients. Another element
which crept in móre than once was the assertion that 'she's not stuck
up', 'she's easy to get on with'; despite the fact that, in many cases,
the volunteer came from a cultural background that would normally
have precluded her from access to the family's home on an informal
basis, she was accepted and appreciated because of her approachable
manner. This was a factor of some importance to many who
compared the volunteer with social workers they had known and
who had been much less attentive and more distant in their manner.
Of course, even with social workers, clients made distinctions within
the breed, referring to them in much the same way as they did with
the volunteers: some were better than others, and some volunteers
were seen as being, not only less useful than social workers, but less
personable as well.

The volunteers were eagerly accepted by this population of clients,
as friends, as social workers, or as something in between. At the
most enthusiastic end of the spectrum Mr Jameson was compared
favourably with the local clergy, and was welcomed for the fact that
he brought an entirely new perspective to Mrs Wise's life; he offered
a different social dimension which the client accepted wholeheartedly
and both found fresh targets for their mutually altruistic natures,
each enjoying the other's company without embarrassment. Similarly,
Mrs Mackintosh was seen as a 'friend and equal'; she overcame the
client's initial apprehension (caused by her previous experience of
social workers and teachers) by virtue of the fact that she was
dressed in almost exactly the same way as the client, and she was
clearly no better off. (Mrs Mackintosh was a student at the time.)
The client liked the ease of communication in the relationship, the

feeling and the understanding that the volunteer was able to convey.

Some of the qualities identified by clients as valued assets are not very different from those which the professional social worker would strive to attain but which, we now know, so often elude him. Maybe warmth, empathy and trust are unachievable except under ideal conditions or in privileged relationships although the best case-workers can undoubtedly still demonstrate them and students can still learn them. But are they really available 'on tap' in the average social worker? Or are they normally confined to interactions which gel, which click, which simultaneously meet ill-defined needs in both client and worker? The evidence from this study is that they, or something like them, are not entirely out of reach of some volunteers, but the suspicion is confirmed that their achievement is relatively rare and not altogether predictable.

What role does the volunteer think he's playing?

We were particularly anxious to identify the critical components of voluntary work, as understood by those most actively involved in it, and so we asked the volunteers to tell us how they thought the families perceived them and what role they thought they were playing in the families' eyes. Clearly the answers given by the volunteers would be an amalgam of their own feelings, their own behaviour and the attitudes and responses of the families they visited. By far the most common word used to describe the volunteer's role was *friend*. 'She (the mother) looks on me as a friend. I'm a lift to them, they know I'm sincere and loyal.' 'They see me as a friend, someone they can talk openly to.' 'a friend, someone who is concerned with her plight'. 'a friend, no questions asked, always made welcome'. In 72 per cent of the research interviews, the word *friend* was used in this manner, and in a further 9 per cent, the same impression was given although the word was not used. However, with a solitary exception, the volunteers' friendly role-playing appeared to preclude any idea of equality in the worker-client relationship. The exception was Mrs Mackintosh who commented that she was in many respects worse off than the client-family; she felt that she got on well with the mother because they saw each other as equals with similar problems and similar stresses. But, in all other cases, there is implicit recognition of the superior position of the volunteer: he sees himself as 'a guide and adviser'; 'the family saw me as someone to help the boy by taking him out'; 'The mother likes me because I'm unpaid—she's surprised that I do it for nothing. She sees me as a stranger to talk to when she's upset'. Frequently and accurately, the volunteer's link with the school was made explicit: 'she's someone from the school', a number of the volunteers were actually introduced to the families by the headmaster as being 'a friend of mine who will come and visit you'; this assertion never seems to have been queried by any of the parties involved, and neither headmaster nor volunteers appeared to recognise anything slightly unusual in the idea of a family accepting without demur intimate and sometimes probing visits from the headmaster's 'friend'.

The volunteers saw their role as a marginal one in the sense that it seemed to take into account the feeling of the families that he was 'on our side' but yet remained a stranger, someone to respect, to defer to, to be grateful to, to admire; three volunteers independently thought they were perceived as a kind of fairy godmother. In perhaps the most enlightening phrase of all, one volunteer captured the role succinctly: 'I think they see me as a friend of the family—an outside friend'. The outside friends varied, of course, in the extent to which they felt their role was accepted wholeheartedly by the family; some had no doubts about the relative intimacy of their position, but others were more doubtful, and their espousal of the friendship role had an element of wishful thinking about it. Those who expressed the most serious doubts about the extent to which they were accepted as friends of the family were indeed those who received the least enthusiastic commendations when we interviewed the clients. To operate successfully as an outside friend appears to depend on the acceptance of one's role by the family itself; to that extent the role is a reciprocal one.

The remaining volunteers (19 per cent) fell into a quite different category which is none the less hinted at in the ambivalent statement of one of the friends, a black volunteer allocated to a black family: 'I felt the mother regarded me as one of her own sort (racially speaking) and this helped me to be accepted by the family. But the mother was undoubtedly still uncertain of my role; she feared I might be spying for the school, but later began to trust me'. In those cases where friendship was not the role, much more negative impressions had been received by the volunteers of the way in which their role was perceived: 'spying for the social services'; 'they see me as just another official'; 'they won't volunteer any information'; 'I'm seen as a visitor rather than a friend—I represent officialdom to them—they're getting more secretive all the time'; 'she saw me as a snooper, she was hostile, resentful and she didn't want me to visit'; 'after an initial welcome, they came to think of me as a nosey-parker —they thought I was investigating'.

As in the survey carried out for the Aves Report, many of the volunteers made a clear distinction between their informal links with the families and what they perceived as the more intrusive operations of the welfare system: 'She knows that I've got no book and pencil, that I'm not going in an official capacity'; 'I'm still trying to gain the confidence of this family—it's important that I'm voluntary, and not an official'. The Aves Report, with its prescriptive task clearly laid down, emphasised the importance of volunteers and professionals each recognising the legitimacy of the other's role, and called on them both to stop being so critical of each other. There is some evidence here, however, that it may be important to recognise when the volunteer is truly an agent of the professionals (as he often is when working for the probation service, for example) and when he is a family's last hope of avoiding the fateful step into the arms of the social services.

This is not to say that the former task precludes the *friendship* role—far from it; but it certainly appears to follow that the volunteer's acceptability will be influenced not only by his mode of approach and his use of personality strengths, but also by the family's present or previous experience of agencies to which the volunteer is thought to be linked. Hence the role of the volunteer can never be defined without sensitive reference both to his organisational base and to the life-style and circumstances of the client to whom he is attached.

Volunteers' assessments of success

We saw in chapter 2 the assessments made by the organiser of the long-term volunteers' work. She indicated that, in her opinion, an overwhelming majority were performing to a high standard, but that rather fewer were making a major impact on the family situation. How do the volunteers themselves judge their work? In discussion with them, much of the emphasis was placed by respondents on their own feelings and experiences; the dominant theme running through almost all the responses was *uncertainty*: uncertainty about role, objectives, and effectiveness. Their responses can be summarised:

  21 per cent were enthusiastic about the work;
  27 per cent were moderately satisfied;
  31 per cent expressed some dissatisfaction;
  21 per cent were very disappointed.

The 21 per cent (N = 7) who were enthusiastic were able to say that they had personally derived immense satisfaction from the Project. Most of them expressed some doubts about its value for the families or the children, but all of them liked to think that they had done something worthwhile. For example, 'I'm very glad I volunteered and I felt it was worthwhile from my point of view; I got a lot out of it. But for the family, I was just another face and a friend.' The volunteer thought it was a bit of a challenge and a good laugh, 'but I felt a bit of an imposter on the school side'. At the time that she severed contact with the family, she felt that her presence had become irrelevant; if she thought that Sharon (the girl to whom she had been attached) had been getting some obvious benefit from the relationship, she'd have stayed on. In the most positive example of all, the volunteer simply said that he wished he had had more time; he would continue his support of Mary even if the Project came to an end, because of the immense satisfaction he had derived from it and because of the help he had been able to give. In a revealing statement, one of the volunteers who felt most enthusiastic about the Project pinpointed a possible reason for others' discontent: 'Personally I don't need feedback. I want to get involved even though I question whether I'm doing any good. But a lack of observable results must discourage many volunteers; feedback does help— you've got to feel you're doing some good.'

Twenty-seven per cent (N = 9) were careful to emphasise that they believed in the value of the Project; they had no regrets about their involvement, and had derived some satisfaction from their work. They had become aware of their own limitations and had learnt to accept them; they tended to practise *low key* activities, expressing patience rather than enthusiasm. All of them expressed doubts about the effectiveness of the Project (as measured against their own expectations and some of the hopes spelt out by the organiser and the headmasters), but most had come to terms with lesser objectives. Many of them had found difficulty in first identifying and then filling their assigned role. They 'couldn't see much else we can do', felt that they hadn't done a lot, didn't particularly enjoy the work at first, but felt a commitment to persevere. One said that she'd had to tread very warily as she had not wished to pry; another wondered whether he was failing or not; and a third indicated that he felt very much an outsider, receiving insufficient feedback from the family about his performance. None the less this group concluded that, on balance, they had enjoyed their involvement with the Project; together with the group of enthusiasts, they made up the 48 per cent who were prepared to judge the Project, and their part in it, a success. Thirty-one per cent of the volunteers (N = 10) told us that they were broadly dissatisfied with their experience of the Project. Some of them were prepared to accept the apparent value of the Project overall, but so far as their role in it was concerned, their feelings were essentially negative. One volunteer, for example, regarded by the organiser and the headmaster as a first-rate recruit, said she was not sorry she had volunteered but she questioned the value of the work. 'I don't feel as if I'm doing anything constructive. It's always in the back of my mind that I can't help her, can't do anything for her.'

A number of the dissatisfied volunteers felt that perhaps the fault lay in the selection of cases, either because they were not in need of help at all or because their problems were too complex. This led some volunteers to suggest that they would be willing to have another try with a different family. Others concentrated their disappointment on their own lack of direction: one said that she'd 'lost sight of the original thing', another that 'the work didn't really fall into place'. This lack of clarity was well expressed by Mrs Silvermann when asked to summarise her role; she said that it was 'a kind of nothingness' and implied that she was glad that she was free of all agency constraints; but as time went by and the problems of the family became more and more severe, the lack of an agency base, the inadequate resources of the Project and the imprecision of the volunteer's objectives—the very *nothingness* element in her work—began to seem unhelpfully sterile; Mrs Silvermann was as active an interventionist as the Project produced, but the multiplicity of crises in terms of accommodation, law-breaking and mental health combined with the shortcomings of the Social Services Department involved in the case proved to be too much for her to cope with. Nobody else in the situation did any better, it is true, but ultimately the Project failed to *support* the child and his family at the crucial times when support was most desperately needed. This was not primarily a failure of the individual volunteer, but rather a structural failure of the Project to fill the critical gaps in community care at an extreme end of the spectrum. We ought not to be surprised by this (especially in the light of recent social work research which highlights the failure of professionals—even when they have reduced caseloads—to do any better), but it is a disappointment to unpaid voluntary personnel to discover that the difficulties they imagined they had been recruited to overcome proved to be too big, too complex or too volatile for them to contain, let alone to solve. Some of them—like Mrs Silvermann—try again but the inevitable tendency is for them to look round for someone to blame—themselves, society, the government or the Project and its failure to train them properly; significantly in this instance nobody blamed the organiser.

The volunteers find it hard to accept that they, like other agents of welfare, get absorbed, to a greater or lesser extent, in client systems of which they have had little experience, and which are unlikely to positively respond to any form of externally imposed intervention; the *moderately satisfied* group had apparently been able to come to terms with their limited role in such a situation, but the *dissatisfied* group (nearly one-third of the whole) were less able to revise their objectives and to accept that they could work only within the context of the family's existing dynamic system. Twenty-one per cent of the group (N = 7) were disappointed to a much more serious extent. One found the whole exercise a very frustrating experience; she never did what she set out to do, never got anywhere; she had hoped to be able to change the childrens' lives and to improve their environment but all she did was to take them out in the car from time to time. Another began to feel angry when she realised that she was 'being used' by the family; she resented the fact that she was denied the right to determine the nature and extent of the help she chose to give, and that the initiative was passing from her to the intended recipients of aid. Three cases combine to illustrate the problem of determining an appropriate target-group: one volunteer complained that the problems in her family's situation were too severe—'any sort of social work is futile, you can't change them'; moreover, she didn't want to probe too deeply for fear of getting over-involved at a time when she had problems enough of her own; the second had left the Project because she was disillusioned with it; 'I was making no impression on them, there seemed no point to it, there was nothing I could do'; this was not because of the severity of the problems, but because she could see no great difficulties to tackle; she couldn't say whether her *failure* as a volunteer was her own fault or that of the family; and the third said quite straight-forwardly that she had found insufficient satisfaction in the work; she preferred 'something more productive—like helping old people'.

Finally, two volunteers were allocated, in succession, to a moderately disturbed boy who was selected by his headmaster as being in need of some stable relationship with an independent adult. His first volunteer, a young married woman, stayed with the Project for fifteen months, and told the organiser that she was leaving only because her husband was changing jobs; however, when we interviewed her, she emerged as being much more critical of the Project than we had expected. She didn't think it was worth-while work; she thought she had done no good at all and was relieved to get away from it since she'd thought she was getting nowhere. The man who succeeded her had been much more open with his feelings. He told us that the Project was a waste of time for him and it had become a source of great personal stress. He had worried endlessly about his efforts and his failure to make progress: 'I was at a loss to know what to do with the kid' and he thought that he might be criticised for making a mess of it.

Achievements and disappointments

A separate attempt was made to secure the volunteers' opinions about their work by asking them to identify any particular achievements or disappointments that they had felt during their time in the Project. First an assessment was made of the balance of replies given:

in 19 instances (58 per cent) it was tipped towards disappointment;
in 12 instances (36 per cent) it was tipped towards a sense of achievement;
in 2 instances (6 per cent) it was evenly balanced.

In a more detailed analysis of the replies, the pattern was confirmed by the fact that fifteen (46 per cent) said that they could identify no felt achievements, while only five (15 per cent) said that they could think of no disappointments. Most of the achievements mentioned were necessarily modest: 'it was an achievement just to form a relationship, to get accepted, and to be there in case I was needed'; 'I hope I've achieved the beginning of a friendship'. Three typically modest answers were 'just being there, just giving help, just listening to the problems'. Altogether ten respondents (30 per cent) identified their achievements primarily in terms of acceptance in the household or of offering their support in a general sense. Twenty-four per cent (N = 8) claimed more concrete results. Two thought they had enabled the families to be more independent, and one had worked as a teaching volunteer in a school: she felt she had been able to help the educational development of the children. A fourth felt that she had helped to give Valerie 'a different sense of her own value, helped her to see herself as normal, and given her some self-confidence'.

The remaining four measured achievements in more material terms: placing the boy in a youth organisation, getting mother a new job, helping the family to pay off rent arrears, providing clothes and a holiday and facilitating a move of house and school. We have already seen that such material aid was by no means rare (see chapter 4) but few of the volunteers identified it as being among their more noteworthy achievements—indeed some of them became critical of their clients if material aid seemed to be developing as a dominant feature in the relationship. Hence, on the whole, the fact that 88 per cent of the volunteers either failed to identify any achievements or mentioned those which were associated with either the interpersonal relationship or with the psychological state of the client-families provides a clear indication of the kind of objectives they had in mind; some who could think of no achievement worth mentioning said they thought they had been inadequately prepared by the Project for the difficulties inherent in offering personal support in the kind of open-ended, undefined way which characterised the original scheme.

What of the disappointments? Five volunteers had not experienced any, although one said it was because she had had no clear idea of what to expect; she'd 'played it by ear and so hadn't felt disappointed when she'd failed to achieve anything very concrete; I felt guilty when I finished but I couldn't cope with school-teaching as well.'

There were two small groups. Three said they were disappointed because the problems presented by their families were so great; they just couldn't do enough to alleviate the social or psychological stress. One of these said she had come in expecting a lot of positive feedback: 'to see working class children developing, and to see the whole problem of social disadvantage in perspective'. She said that she did indeed get a lot out of her work—'more than I expected'—but she was disappointed at the lack of movement in the situation.

Three others were frustrated by a lack of co-operation from other personnel. One was annoyed with the headmaster for refusing to let her work with the family at home—he wanted her to concentrate her efforts on the school premises; and the other two found themselves frustrated by what they saw as a lack of co-operation from the Social Services Department.

But two thirds of all the disappointments (N = 22) reflected the critical interaction between the personal feelings and motivations of the volunteers and the structural objectives and limitations of the Project. A distressingly large number of the volunteers brought enthusiasm, optimism and commitment to their work but found that these were sooner or later dissipated in the vagueness of the Project's *Support* objective, in the sheer practical difficulty of breaking into the family system in which they had been asked to operate and in the ongoing task of giving help as an outside friend whose presence might often be suspect and who could and did choose to opt out of the 'friendship' after a couple of months or a couple of years. Volunteers speak of their lack of expertise and their lack of confidence to tackle the complex situations that confronted them. Mrs Bowers felt 'disappointed with her own performance. You have to be so damn tactful with them'. She dislikes the 'snooping role' which she says the head has given her. Mrs Chappell is mainly disappointed that the Project lacks clarity in its objectives. One thought the Project would be 'more demanding', while another was sad that she had not been able to establish a working relationship with a child as she had hoped. Most disturbing of all, however, is the way in which many of the volunteers express real personal concern about their failure, and often blame themselves:

Mrs Slasberg thought the family was pleased with her friendship at first, but became increasingly disappointed with her apparent inability to get through to them. She blamed herself for using the wrong approach.

Miss Worrall was disappointed with herself: 'I wanted more out of what I was doing—I didn't think I'd done enough for them.'

Mrs Eaton felt she'd helped by giving the family a sense of

independence. 'I couldn't have done much more, but I must be one of those people who soon get disheartened.' She felt she had outlived her usefulness with the family.

Miss Clinton felt disappointed with herself in that she thought she wasn't doing enough for the family. 'I really expected to find more solid problems that I could tackle. It was like walking into a brick wall which then evaporated before my eyes.' She thought that the lack of feedback from the family led very quickly to a feeling of disillusionment.

These are not the detached opinions of respondents taking a cool look at situations outside their sphere of interest; they are the emotive expressions of real disappointment. The volunteers were clearly achieving less, much less, than they had anticipated when they responded to the Project's call. What then do the families think?

Families' judgment of the Project

The families' judgment of the Project is, of course, a judgment of the role played and the relationship established by a single individual.

We saw earlier that families were by no means overwhelmingly hostile to the volunteers. As many as 70 per cent spoke to us of their varying degrees of positive feeling towards the individuals who had visited them. But how useful did they think the Project had been? Assessments were made on a five-point scale:

  5 (15 per cent) said the volunteers had been of maximum value;
  9 (26 per cent) said the volunteers had been of considerable value;
  13 (38 per cent) said the volunteers had been of marginal value;
  6 (18 per cent) said the volunteers had served no purpose;
  1 (3 per cent) alleged that the volunteer had been worse than useless.

A group of five spoke of the volunteers, not merely in terms of glowing praise, but in a manner which suggested that the volunteer had played a crucially important role in the family situation: two mentioned help given to clients who had been contemplating suicide during periods of deep depression, while the other three volunteers were referred to in different terms as substitute parents, functioning in either supportive or controlling roles for the benefit of the child. At a less significant, but still useful level, twenty-two volunteers are listed as having been of either considerable or marginal value in the eyes of their families. Their role was identified in specific terms: the giving of financial or material aid, filling in forms for grants or social security, helping around the house, taking children out to football matches, to picnics or to the shops or guiding the children with their leisure-time activities. Additionally, most respondents commented on the value of being able to talk openly, easily, and in confidence to the volunteer.

To some extent the first group of five reflects the difficult circumstances of the situation in which the volunteers found themselves as well as their own particular skills and contributions; but in all the cases in which the volunteers were perceived as having been useful to some degree, two elements emerge as being important: first, and in the very traditional social work mould, it is apparent that *the quality of the relationship* established is a prerequisite of success. The positive respondents talk of the ease with which they could converse with the volunteer, his surprising accessibility, his trustworthiness and commitment; in other, less positive cases, comment is made on the fact that an initial friendliness was later belied by the ease with which the volunteer chose to withdraw, or his failure to fulfil earlier expectations. Secondly, there is the ability of the volunteer to come up with *help seen to have been of practical (not necessarily material) value*. The most contented recipients of aid could quickly point to events or experiences which they thought reflected useful work done by the volunteer, often including verbal support which was frequently mentioned as an important element in the volunteer's contribution to their lives.

Where the usefulness of the volunteer was questioned or derided by a family, the criticism tended to reflect his failure to come up to the client's expectations in these two areas: first, there were some who were said to have never developed a close working relationship (sometimes because of the age difference between them and the schoolchildren to whom they had been attached), others were criticised for not persisting long enough in the contact or for being deterred by their own inexperience or hesitance, and one was said to have been too talkative; second, a common complaint by critics was that they were less efficient in practice than social workers because they didn't have access to adequate resources, and could only act as middlemen or advocates on behalf of the clients whereas the professionals were perceived as being resource-agents in their own right.

When the families' criteria for usefulness are identified in this way — a good relationship plus something of practical value to offer — we can see again the heavy responsibility that is placed on the shoulders of inexperienced volunteers in an open-ended project such as this. In this light it becomes important to recognise the surprising nature of some of the volunteers' successes, rather than the all-too-predictable quality of their disappointments.

Conclusion

Where then does the balance of judgment rest? The picture is far from simple, not only because there is discrepancy between the volunteers' own assessments and those of the families to whom they were attached, but also because the pattern is known to change during the course of a relationship (a fact that we have not been able to take fully into account during this study) and because descriptions of past experiences and previous feelings are notoriously vulnerable to distortion. All we can do is reflect the moods of the respondents to our interviews at the time we met them, and to try to capture the total picture that is there to be portrayed; in order to do this, the relatively small-sized population of volunteers is far from being a disadvantage, because although, for convenience, we have reduced a limited number of statements to percentage-form, the main silhouette that emerges from the study can be made to mirror the total set of impressions that the interviews created for the researcher.

It has to be concluded that more good than harm came out of the Project. The gratitude of five families for the intensive, committed help of outside friends who, but for the Project, would have remained unknown to them cannot be denied; nor can one ignore the testimony of others who spoke of 'the good influence', 'the provision of much needed pleasure' or the patient provision of practical aid in times of need. The fact that many families thought it worthy of comment that their volunteers were not snobbish, stuck up or proud, may to some seem irrelevant or even regrettable, but that does not detract from the obvious joy they derived at receiving visits from people they respected.

The Project did not have objectives which enabled us to identify criteria by which it could be judged, and certainly it would have been excessively optimistic (as it has proved in many social work experiments) to look for achievements such as reductions in truancy or delinquency, and improvements in the employment rate for school-leavers; although there were individual cases in which families, volunteers and headmasters all claimed some such benefit, the data are not such as to enable any evaluative judgment to be made in areas such as these. If there were gains of this kind, they were very marginal.

The most surprising aspect of the work lies in the apparent discrepancy between the families' view and that of the volunteers themselves. It is valid to conclude that, on balance, there was more satisfaction among the families than among the volunteers; four-fifths of the families were able to speak, with varying degrees of enthusiasm, about the usefulness of their volunteers, while less than

63

half of the volunteers were, on balance, satisfied with their efforts and the outcome. The most surprising aspect of our interviews, coming, as they did, after the largely optimistic conclusions drawn from the preliminary monitoring exercise (reported in chapters 1 and 2), was the underlying feeling of disappointment that characterised the majority of the comments we received from the volunteers. Almost certainly they had brought to their work more ambitious expectations than were justified by the reality-situations confronting them, and they had probably held more hope of change than most of the families knew to be feasible; the problem here, as in social work generally, is the question of whether such optimism and hope are necessary to the recruitment of personnel, or whether it is possible to persuade people to operate in an altogether lower key. Certainly the successes in the Project stem not from high expectations, but rather from persistence and patience, from a warm sympathetic and tolerant attitude towards the misfortunes of others, and from the self-confidence, discipline, and, to some extent, the experience of volunteers who were able to offer a framework within which a new, unequal but none the less reciprocal relationship could be developed. To achieve this success, the input of effort was relatively heavy, and one cannot avoid wondering whether the same or better results might be achieved through the medium of a less cumbersome superstructure with more precise objectives; before considering this question further, it is important to record that, judged primarily by consumer opinion, the Support Project has to be counted successful. The lesser enthusiasm of many of the volunteers is a separate issue which will be discussed again in the next chapter.

Chapter six

Volunteers in their social context

The Aves Report (1969) made a brave attempt to differentiate the respective roles of volunteers and professionals in the practice of social work; that the result remains unconvincing is a reflection, not so much of the vagueness of aims and policies which characterise the voluntary sector, as of the corresponding imprecision which is the hallmark of statutory social work, and which is best reflected in the discrepancies which exist between the public expectations of social services departments and the actual functioning of their employees. Aves asserts on two separate occasions (ibid., pp. 86, 183) that 'volunteers should not be regarded as substitutes for professional workers' and it can be argued that, with regard to such statutory functions as decision-making, the exercise of social control and report-writing, a paid employee is the only person who can be held fully responsible by a government organisation, but in such areas as counselling, the provision of generalised support, the assessment of needs and planning programmes of help in association with the client, the distinction is almost certainly not between the trained professional and the volunteer, but between different levels of skill and ability some of which derive from learning and experience, and some of which may reflect individual strengths of personality.

It is perhaps significant that the Aves Report quotes the skills of nurses and youth leaders in arguing that it would be unrealistic for organisations to expect volunteers to function as effectively as professionals. Unfortunately for social workers, in many of the functions traditionally, if sometimes wrongly, associated with social work, the qualities required are not primarily professional at all and it only serves, and has served, to bring social work into disrepute if other groups are denied the right to demonstrate their abilities in areas which are traditionally concerned with the normal processes of human interaction—involving empathy, commitment and love.

Much social work, in both the local authorities and in probation, is slowly changing its identity, and those employed in the service of the state are having to recognise that, whatever their own original views, they are paid to serve society first and their clients only when society identifies them as being in need of social work intervention. The provision of support services in the community on anything like the scale which appears to be needed is going to depend on an extension of the voluntary commitment; far too little is known about the indigenous support systems functioning in society, or about the relationship of organised volunteer schemes to them, but we must presumably accept an increasing degree of social and geographical mobility in urban Britain, and with it a concomitant degree of network disruption. Policies involving rehousing, job mobility, inter-generational drift, and the shift from burgher-employment to spirallist-employment all suggest that local authorities might have to accept a responsibility to offer systems of oversight in the community in order to ensure the standards of social living to which increased affluence in society entitles every citizen.

If this is so, then perhaps we ought to think much more clearly about the need to allocate volunteers to defined geographical areas; at the moment, their distribution is haphazard. If there is a belief in their potential value in a wide range of settings, it would be possible to argue that the most appropriate link-up would be between voluntary work and community work. Certainly, as social workers become more specialised (*pace* Seebohm Report, 1968), more concerned with decision-making and resource allocation, less linked with small geographical areas, more prone to movement around the country and to rapid promotion, then the role for voluntary workers would seem to be potentially more valuable if they could be attached to a geographical entity. 'Since voluntary workers do not need to concern themselves with administrative distinctions they can ignore the boundaries between services, and concentrate on human needs' (Aves, op. cit., p. 23). This may be an over-simplification in the present context in which volunteers are seen as no more than accessories to the bureaucrats, but in a radical new setting the volunteers might become recognised as community leaders, and be appointed by their own community sector.

Motivation of the volunteers

The Aves Report identified three elements in the complex motivation patterns which bring volunteers into operation: altruism, self-interest and sociability. 'Only a few mentioned religious beliefs as their motives for doing voluntary work, but it cannot be assumed from this that such beliefs play only a small part in the motivation of volunteers.' Our discussions with volunteers in the Support Project revealed two further factors which appeared to be of significance: 48 per cent of the volunteers had ambitions to move into social work full-time, although a considerable proportion of these had already suffered set-backs in their applications, usually because of age or their lack of educational qualifications; and 64 per cent told us that the Support Project was by no means their first foray into voluntary activities. Indeed their previous experience was impressive: fostering, Samaritans, extensive involvement with religious charities, hospital voluntary work, all these and more were present in the background of the volunteers. At one point the organiser commented on the surprising fact that the majority of those who stayed with the Project and became long-term operators were the ones who appeared at first sight to be already over-committed in other directions.

If the two groups are added together (and allowing for the overlap), it means that 82 per cent of the total had either voluntary work or social work experience or had social work aspirations; for them, the Project was not something beyond their range of experience. It conformed to the pattern of their lives either as they had already experienced it or as they would have liked it to evolve in the future.

To identify motives is a complex task, and cannot be achieved to any sophisticated extent by the methods used either by the Aves Committee or in the present study. But it does seem to be important to recognise that, when we are talking about social work volunteers, we are almost certainly concerned with a fairly specific population whose mental and social lives have already brought them into range of this type of activity. This is not to argue that there is a volunteer-type of person (although in common parlance, people might suspect that there is), but that at any point in time, there is probably a limited population from which the normal body of volunteers might be drawn; it is as much a sociological fact as a psychological one.

This point is given further emphasis by looking more closely at the altruism on which Aves comments and which certainly drew in a considerable proportion of the Support Project volunteers. Altogether two-thirds of the people gave answers which indicated their essentially altruistic motivation, but again the responses are significant for the light they throw on the volunteers' previous experiences. Twenty-four per cent, for example, had had close family experience with an ESN child and said they had been lucky in the help they had received; now they wanted to repay some of the debt that they felt they owed to society; others spoke of their identification with the misfortunes of others, because of their own impoverished or suffering childhood, because of physical pain they had experienced or because of their awareness of the privileged position they held with a happy family and material comforts.

Significantly, perhaps, in a Project which required its volunteers to work on their own, no one mentioned their need for companionship as a motive for coming into the work; presumably those would be among the earliest drop-outs. Only 36 per cent spoke openly about their own personal needs at all, although as we have already argued, it is clear that personal satisfaction from the work was an almost essential prerequisite for all. Perhaps the best example of this group was the Assistant Governor in the prison service who found that the desk-bound nature of his job meant that he had fewer personal contacts than he had hoped for; accordingly he looked to the Support Project to provide him with the opportunity to keep in touch with ordinary people in a helping capacity. Others spoke simply of the gratification they obtained from doing some form of personal service; as Aves comments, 'there is no reason to deprecate the fact that volunteers do find some of their own needs fulfilled through the work which they do' (ibid., p. 43).

The motives which lead people to apply to become volunteers, to persevere through the initial stages, and then to keep going for one, two or more years are extremely complex. Certainly there must be personality factors involved, but once recruited, there are likely to be more complex interactionist elements in the social situation in which they find themselves. These involve the client-family to which they are attached, the school and its headmaster, social workers and other related professionals with whom they may come into contact or even into conflict, the organiser and, perhaps of major significance, their own families and, if applicable, their occupations. In other words, it is quite wrong and misleading to think of the relationship between volunteer and client as a social artifact in isolation from the community in which both play their part. If either underestimate the importance of the other's social situation or of the social determinants likely to affect them both in the wider society it seems likely that the contact will prove to be as sterile as we now know the majority of routine professional social work contacts are. The great asset of the volunteer is not just time, as Aves suggests, but his ability to become involved in the life of the client (which admittedly needs time—but it isn't time which is the vital factor). The volunteer brings with him his previous experiences and his present circumstances, he contributes to the client's life his own feelings and perceptions; the closer the two become, the more impact will the volunteer's own life-setting have on the client's situation. That the essential inequality remains in most cases is undeniable, but the volunteer gradually allows the client to enter into *his* own situation and so to influence it in turn. The support process becomes more dynamic in its implications, provided the client and the volunteer equally allow it to develop; both have the power to prevent this happening, both can maintain maximum formality, but few of the situations lend themselves to such restrictive policies over a long period of time: either the relationship evolves, or it comes to an end. Hence the personal involvement and commitment of the volunteer are tested, and only those willing to engage in such dynamics persist in their work; the relationship becomes an important segment in both client's and volunteer's continuing experience.

Paradox of supportive social work

It was suggested in chapter 2 that, once in post, the volunteers worked in relative isolation from the Project and the school, and created an autonomous relationship with the client-family to which they had been attached. In the sense that they became responsible for their own supportive activities, this is true, but it does not follow that they were working in a social vacuum. They retained links with the organiser and the headmasters, and they tended to draw on contacts with other people too; indeed, it can be argued that the most successful volunteers were those who most effectively became involved in wider groupings involving themselves and the clients, the ones who established the most informal relationships, and took the most active part in the clients' own environment: Valerie Schofield played it by ear and enjoyed it; she liked Janet's company and that of her widower-father, and became a friend of the family. She didn't try to do anything extraordinary or to tackle anything she couldn't handle. She helped Janet through school-leaving and into work, and they became close friends; they went swimming, boating, shopping and out to school functions. Janet's father tended to dominate the conversation at home, and Valerie got on well with him too; she went out for a drink a couple of times with him, and almost became part of the family. She gave him some guidance with money problems, but found that, on the whole, the family was coping well. After twelve months, Valerie decided that her presence had become largely irrelevant; Janet was settled into work, and it seemed a convenient time to break; none the less, she felt very guilty when she finished, but realised that her own time and energy were limited. In retrospect, she's not sure that the family really needed a volunteer; Valerie herself says she got a lot out of it—it was 'a bit of a challenge, a bit of fun, an ego-booster', but she wonders whether, to Janet and her father, she was not just another face and a friend. The clients, in interview, confirm the quality of the friendship they'd experienced, but also say that Valerie had been very helpful during the time that she had visited them; they liked her.

Hence Valerie Schofield *was* 'another face, another friend'. The family didn't seem to need more, but all three parties appreciated the value of what they experienced. It is one of the most troublesome paradoxes about supportive social work that cases in which support is successfully given often appear in retrospect to have been those in which it was superfluous, while those cases in which resistance is apparent, or the worker rejected, seem to be the very ones in need of intervention and support.

Volunteers and professionals

It had originally been planned that volunteers would not be attached to families already in touch with the social services department, but in practice this intention was not fulfilled. There were cases which headmasters identified as being obvious candidates for allocation to volunteers who none the less had had dealings with social workers in the recent past; in very few cases, however, was there a close relationship existing at the time the volunteer was referred. However, in the majority of situations social workers were, or had been, involved and some attempt was made to tap the attitudes of both families and volunteers towards the social services. In nineteen out of the thirty-three cases, social workers of one kind or another were known to be involved or to have been involved at some time in the past; in most instances, the involvement had been apparently peripheral or short-lived, but in a few supervision had been more intensive. In twelve of these cases, the volunteers had come into contact with the social workers either directly or indirectly, and had formed opinions which they expressed to us about the performance of the social workers. Two volunteers were favourably disposed towards the work of the social services but six were markedly critical; another three expressed opinions which could be categorised as deferential 'I wouldn't want to tread on the social worker's toes.'; one was non-committal. Conversely there is evidence to suggest that some of the social workers treated the volunteers rather dismissively, although others were prepared to see value in voluntary work; the majority were probably unaware of the volunteers' existence. All these circumstances have already been recognised and documented by Aves: the committee found that social workers had mixed feelings about the value of volunteers, but that volunteers found their greatest frustrations occurring in their relationships with professional staff. 'Volunteers were found to be consistent on the whole . . . in their somewhat unflattering opinions of professional workers, whom they tended to see as rigid, inhuman, "official" in their attitude, and doing their work "simply as a job"' (ibid., p. 47). Not unnaturally, Aves thought it important to give some thought to the reasons 'for the very widespread denigration of officials', and tentatively concluded that these might be found in the rejecting attitude of social workers towards the volunteers, in the tendency for volunteers to over-identify with their clients and therefore to attack agency professionals for being hostile, and especially in the lack of clarity in the volunteer's role leading them to seek clarification by distinguishing their natural warmth from the officials' bureaucratic distance. These three factors may all be present, but they seem to ignore what is almost certainly the major factor: it is not so much the lack of clarity in the volunteer's role as the lack of clarity in the social workers' objectives that creates difficulties—at any rate in such a project as the Support Project, in which the volunteers are functioning in a helping way quite divorced from the mainstream task of the social services. It is not so much that volunteers are wrong to criticise social workers for 'just doing a job in which they have no real interest' (ibid., p. 52), or that social workers are wrong 'who consider that voluntary workers are essentially undependable'; it is rather that the job which social workers are increasingly required to do reflects aspects of social control, resource allocation and decision-making which take them further and further away from the traditional helping, supportive view of social work which volunteers understand, which some professionals yearn for (and in privileged situations may still be able to practise) but which is unlikely ever to be fulfilled again at a professional level; similarly, it would seem to suggest that the selection, briefing and supervision of volunteers becomes crucially important if they are to be used for such demanding tasks as characterised the Support Project's objectives, and if they are to be perceived by the community, the professions and the administration with the same degree of respect and admiration as most of them earned from the Support Project clients. Aves talks wistfully of the possibility of narrowing the gulf between volunteers and paid workers so that each side can begin to perceive more realistically that contribution which the other makes (ibid., p. 52); but it is not a question of narrowing the gulf; what is needed is the clarification of objectives and the preparation of each side more appropriately to attain their respective goals. If that is done, then greater respect becomes possible; the danger arises only if the professional social worker actively resents the volunteer or the community representative taking upon himself some of the more attractive tasks that have erstwhile been the fantasised segment of social work practice; it is the social worker who must come to terms with the increasingly specialised and target centred nature of his

71

work; the ongoing support of individuals at risk or of families in need may come to be seen as an inappropriate function for the local authority social worker to perform.

Rounded perspective

For a long time, many social scientists argued that the most accurate way of undertaking research involved large samples and numerical analysis; there is no denying the value of such methods, but they alone provide a limited perspective. Especially when the area of investigation involves complex patterns of social interaction there is a growing recognition that quantitative methods, requiring the reduction of social and psychological reality to a crude form, may be inferior to apparently less reliable observations of a small number of total situations. The larger the sample, the less easy it is to allow for multiple variations in relationships (even with the use of sophisticated techniques of electronic data processing); but the more detail one sees in a few examples of social reality, the less typical the observations may be. In the present instance, it is clear that the simplistic extrapolation of facts and figures about different attitudes does no more than whet the appetite for further analyses of the interactions between volunteers, clients and social workers.

There is no predominant pattern, but in each case, the various parties' reactions reflected their personalities, their formal role-playing and status, their current motivations and moods, and the effect of each on the other. It is this kind of circumstance which has so often led social workers to react angrily against researchers with the accusation that they tend to oversimplify reality, and consequently purvey untruths. Certainly the researcher can throw light on behaviour by his view from outside, but he can also distort it if he seeks to impose too all-encompassing an interpretation on behaviour which denies the validity of experience as it is felt by those involved. Our interviews threw further light on the experience that families had had with social workers, and they cast strong doubt on the concept of professionalism as it has been traditionally understood. The most positive comments made by some of the families are of two kinds: firstly, recognition is given to the social worker's readier access to material resources and to the seats of local authority power (e.g. in housing); by contrast many of the volunteers were commended for their efforts, but their weak position was acknowledged. And secondly, selected social workers were praised for their *personal* qualities—their accessibility, friendliness, helpfulness and sympathy. These then were elements that reflected social work as teachers and administrators have always liked to imagine it: operating from a strong and relevant agency base, and practised by individuals whose professionalism enabled them to relate to clients in need, not necessarily to respond, but at least to achieve understanding. Unfortunately such qualities were rarely identified. Instead, and more often, families mentioned less attractive individual and agency characteristics: difficulty in communicating with social workers; the fact that they (the clients) had always to do the pushing, the prompting, the asking, the chasing; their feeling of social workers' snooping on them; and, perhaps most commonly, their view of social workers as condescending bureaucrats, flaunting their status and their superiority, putting the client in his place, making him feel inadequate.

When we turned to look more closely at the volunteers' comments on the social workers, we found similar reactions (not altogether surprisingly, perhaps, as some of them were indeed reflecting the clients' versions of their experience, although many of the volunteers also had had dealings with the professionals). The majority of the volunteers expressed general admiration of social work as a profession and some of them, as we have seen, aspired to enter it. But they too differentiated clearly between individuals, complained of having to push social workers into activity, of being treated as second-class citizens when communicating with social workers until their status was established. In addition, they added the criticism that too many social workers were over-theoretical, even over-intellectual, and had inadequate sensitivity to the harsher realities of everyday living in an urban situation. Significantly, where clients commented negatively on the volunteers it was either because of their shortcomings as a resource-agent or because they were no easier to communicate with than the typical social workers; when social workers were selected for praise, it was either because of their practical helpfulness, or, more often, because they were seen as being unusually approachable and friendly—like the majority of the volunteers. On the other hand, it should be borne in mind that this demand on the volunteers for accessibility and friendliness did sometimes become something of a burden, and the question of how long the role can be fulfilled, outside of either a personal relationship of a mutually selected and mutually rewarding kind or a fully professional relationship is of crucial significance.

We see reflected here the three different social systems: that of the client, who may look for help, but will settle for a relationship in which he is treated as a fully-fledged, self-respecting individual; that of the volunteer, whose facility to help may be limited—depending on his declared function—but who seems to be exceptionally able to offer a human relationship which the client accepts, understands and appreciates; and that of the social worker, whose resources are not insignificant, but are none the less rationed, and whose capacity for providing personal help through an ongoing relationship is now known to be at least restricted and sometimes nonexistent and for whom agency pressures, large caseloads, confused working objectives, and personal shortcomings appear to have had a damaging effect on his capacity to offer a warm, friendly, respectful, persona despite the fact that his motives may be beyond reproach and despite any training he may have received in the past. Indeed the evidence from this study is that training does not appear to be the main vehicle for achieving an essentially empathetic relationship; for, if professionalism means anything in social work, it must mean the ability to function at the highest possible level especially with regard to human relationships, and the ability to offer a respectful relationship even against the odds, even, for example, when agency pressures are high, when caseload turnover is rapid, and when client hostility is predictable. Too much emphasis has been placed on the concept of professionalism being no more than a passport to occupational respectability, without adequate recognition of the implications that it carries; if it is impossible in the statutory sector to run a service which can guarantee a performance offering respect for the client, respect which the client himself experiences, then the idea of a professional social service has indeed become a mockery. For in this study, the volunteers, for all their shortcomings, emerged on balance in the eyes of the clients as being more respected counsellors than the professionals.

There is widespread recognition of the need to clarify the statutory social worker's role, and the process of clarification is already in motion. But there is also a need to clarify our society's need for support systems in the community, and it seems, on present evidence, unlikely that social workers will ever be able to meet those needs except in the most marginal, transient and arbitrary circumstances. If that is so, then it follows that a caring society must make a large-scale commitment to community care by harnessing voluntary resources in a fashion hitherto unimagined in the Western world. Of course no society can ever hope to meet all the needs of its people, but it is apparent that much more could be done, especially in the disrupted cities and towns of today. We need to face up to the question, 'Is such a support system viable even for the volunteer?' Aves, in effect, says 'No'; volunteers should only be used with precise functions, as for example in literacy schemes or to provide outings or transport for visits to relatives. And the drop-out rate reported in chapters 1 and 2 is certainly a factor to take into account; but, conversely there is evidence that with a more structured setting, some increased supervision, and a clearer *raison d'être*, more volunteers could be recruited to function to provide support in a generalised sense. Certainly, the majority of the client-families valued it, said they were glad of the opportunity to contact the volunteer in case of need, and hinted that this way of operating might perhaps have considerable potential as a preventative measure.

Volunteers and the schools

We have already discussed in chapter 3 the varying attitudes of the headmasters towards the volunteers. But when we came to interview, first the volunteers, and then the families we found almost complete unanimity in their expressions of positive opinions about the schools, the headmasters, the teachers, the learning opportunities and the educational regimes as a whole. All the volunteers except one spoke in admiration of the schools; the exception was a man who thought that the headmaster had not understood the needs of the child allocated to him. Three typical responses were:

'The headmaster is helpful, welcoming, very open. I think it's wonderful. There's no jealousy at all. I've worked in situations where there would have been far more resentment at the intrusion of amateurs.'

'I feel as though I'm part of the school. Mr Jevons is marvellous.'

'The atmosphere is excellent. The headmaster is very relaxed, informal, down-to-earth, caring. He treats me not quite like a colleague—after all, he *is* a professional—but he's not condescending.'

Among the families, the same kind of words recurred: 'marvellous, very understanding, nice'. And the majority of parents expressed appreciation of the help their child or children had received. A minority of eight (24 per cent) were critical, several because of the alleged 'hardness' of one teacher towards the kids, especially when they truanted. One mother commented that the school seemed to have had little understanding of the specialised needs of autistic children; the parents who were totally hostile towards their volunteer were equally critical of the school and its teachers; and three felt that the school had been less helpful or sympathetic to their needs than it might have been.

What is immediately striking from the interviews focused on the schools, however, apart from the high degree of satisfaction, is the status distance of the ties: both volunteers and families accepted the innate superiority and authority of the schools and especially of the heads, expressed gratitude for such time as they were given, and admired the professional skills of the teachers both in educational terms and in their handling of external visitors like the volunteers and the families. This is not to imply criticism of the situation, but rather to emphasise that it highlights the qualitative difference, the closeness, and the greater emotional intensity of the volunteer-client relationship; this, as we argued earlier took on an existence all its own. The schools were powerful institutions who had engineered the relationship, but who remained on its periphery once it was established. They did not, for the most part, participate in it except as an absent influence: the stresses and strains were hopefully delegated to the new system—otherwise, as Mr Behrens said, if the families still come to the school for a shoulder to cry on, or if the volunteers need close supervision by the head (as distinct from a home-school liaison teacher, whose job it was), why bother with such an arrangement at all?

As one of the headmasters argued at the launching of the scheme in 1971, the aim is to delegate responsibility for family-child problems that have some spill-over into the educational situation (or which the teachers are simply in a position to identify) to an additional resource. This resource must, according to Mr Jevons remain firmly under the control of the school: 'If anyone else—the Social Services Department, for example—muscled in on my volunteers, I just wouldn't want to know any more, it's as simple as that; they must be responsible to the headmaster'. Other headmasters were not quite so dogmatic as this, but all identified the need as deriving very much from the universally alleged inadequacies of the Social Services Department whose staff were not trusted by the schools to provide the kind of counselling facility needed; moreover, all the headmasters had tales to tell of the Department failing even to respond to crisis situations reported to them from the school.

At the time of the Project, discussions were beginning—in the wake of the Colwell Enquiry Report (DHSS, 1974), which criticised the poor communications between social workers and teachers—which, it was hoped, would improve matters so far as Manchester's special schools were concerned. But, even with hoped-for improvements in the staffing and other resources of the Social Services Departments, it was clear that all the headmasters were anxious to develop their own social education facility, to extend the appointment of home-school liaison teachers and to continue to use volunteers in increased numbers—perhaps, in some cases, for more specific tasks but also for the type of counselling and support service that the Support Project had pioneered.

This, then, brings us to the point of identifying the complex circumstances that surround the helping process. At first sight it is a simple matter to talk of identifying needs among families and children, and then of allocating suitable volunteers to meet those needs. In some projects—as, for example, with the elderly studied by Hadley and Webb, or with prisoners' wives who benefit from transport facilities provided by voluntary associates attached to the probation service—such marrying of demand and supply may be easily achieved, although even here, the reality is not always so straightforward; but in the Support Project we are brought face to face with an aspect of social work that has dominated thinking in the profession for many years: how feasible is it to provide long-term community care of a generalised kind? In this Project, we are able to identify the elements which have lately led social workers and theorists to argue that such aspirations are unrealistic and that the professionals should concentrate on task-centred casework, on short-term or crisis care, and should disavow any attempt to provide pastoral care of the conventional kind. And yet, in contradistinction to this, the need for such care among the deprived seems to be as great as ever or greater and the demand for it from related professionals and other interested parties is no less intense. The time has come for society to decide whether it is a legitimate part of its social policy to organise a system of meeting such needs and, if so, how it can be organised democratically, without creating an elephantine bureaucratic structure, and in such a way as to tap the enormous reservoir of volunteer commitment in the community.

We have seen in our portrayal of the helping process:
(a) Disagreement among the headmasters as to the kind of help they require for their schools, their families and their children. Disagreement among them, too, as to the volume of unmet need among their families, the capacity of volunteers to meet that need and the appropriate form of relating volunteers to the structure of the school.
(b) The difficulty of recruiting a sufficient number of volunteers, and of keeping them committed to the Project, of ensuring their satisfaction with the work and their satisfactory performance of the task.
(c) The reality of status differentials among the various parties involved: clients-volunteers, volunteers-schools, schools-social services, volunteers-social services and the effect this has on the smooth running and effectiveness of the volunteer's performance.
(d) The type of organisational strategy adopted by the agency and the schools, the degree of supervision provided, the guidelines adopted, and the objectives identified.
(e) The confused concept of professionalism and the extent to which it is suggested that there are certain activities normally considered to be beyond the scope of the volunteer.
(f) The extent to which the helping process is identified as being concerned with precise tasks or with the provision of generalised support.

77

(g) The trend in social services and probation departments to emphasise task-centred, short-term approaches contrasted with the still apparent need in society for a caring commitment to those in need. Increasingly difficult to meet professionally—especially as statutory agencies move swiftly into the predominant areas of social control, resource allocation and decision-making—society is faced with the question of how best it is to be attempted. Is it something which society should consider organising anyway? Can volunteers play a part? If so, should they be under the direction of the statutory services? Or should some measure of autonomy and independence be preserved? Can the provision be made on a piecemeal, problem-centred basis, or should it be blanketed into the community superstructure?

These are the questions to which our turbulent, plural society must turn. For just as volunteers must be viewed in the context of their lives as a whole—both in the past and the present—so too must clients and social workers, teachers and administrators sometimes be seen as a part of the wider fabric of society. Of course, it is extremely difficult to analyse social interactions in all their complexity, but the society in which the social worker operates and for which the politician legislates and the administrator plans is necessarily complex and will become more so, and the exploration of a concept like that of *helping* in modern urban society is bound to involve some attempt to observe the interactions at work. It is because of this that systems theory has been suggested as offering the possibility of moving beyond the level of naive assertions and would-be aspirations to the point where we can begin to truly understand the nature of the processes occurring and set them in a framework which might enable us to plan their development and assess their value as a part of the social and educational facilities in the community.

Part three

Systems theory and social work

Chapter seven

Background to systems theory

Introduction

Despite the frequent use of the phrase 'case-work theory' the social work profession has never been wholly persuaded of the appropriateness of any one theoretical approach. Even during the years when Freudian thinking was at its most pervasive, there is evidence that *practising* social workers employed a more pragmatic approach to their work than was usually admitted; in the areas of child care, probation and psychiatric and medical social work (i.e. in the pre-Seebohm mainstream) the psychoanalytic foundations of case-work teaching were often undermined or at least amended by the realities of the here-and-now situation in practice. Moreover, in all other areas of social work—with the handicapped and the elderly, in the schools and in residential care—the influence of Freudian theory was minimal. And it is one of the ironies of British social work in the 1970s that, although one of the expectations of Seebohm was that the mainstream of social work theory should be given the opportunity to exercise its influence over the less 'enlightened' areas of practice, the effect of re-organisation has been at least as powerful in the reverse direction: many traditionally trained social workers have had to come to terms with the fact that much of their work now involves social relations with clients and their environments of such a kind that case-work theory derived principally from ego-psychology must take its place alongside other influential frameworks drawn from behaviourism, sociology, organisational theory and penal theory. When the role of the social worker is increasingly caught up in decision-making, the allocation of scarce resources and the exercise of social control, it is apparent that ego-psychology, though relevant, is only one aspect of the theoretical armour required. Even in probation, which had looked as though it might continue to enjoy its reputation as the last bastion of mainstream traditional case-work, it is now clear that the pressures of parliament and public opinion are requiring officers to consider the equally important contributions to be made from behaviourism and learning theory.

In the light of this, and in order to overcome the dangers of adopting a purely cafeteria approach to social work theory, 'take what you like and use it as you wish', a number of tentative attempts have been made in recent years to devise a more all-embracing theoretical framework. As yet, these attempts have to be recognised as being at a relatively premature stage of development; despite their interest and usefulness, none of them has yet convincingly provided a comprehensive theoretical alternative. Indeed, such is the variety of social work settings now and such is the range of objectives and of functions that it seems increasingly less appropriate to maintain the belief that there is any such thing as a social work theory *per se*. There are theoretical contributions to social work knowledge, but their appropriateness may not be of equal weight in different situations or with different clients; thus the work of a private agency family counsellor in San Francisco, a British probation officer responsible for supervising a recidivist-parolee, a local authority social worker allocating aids to the handicapped and a school counsellor recommending residential care for a persistent truant covers a wide range of roles, in all of which a variety of theoretical perspectives is likely to be relevant and influential.

Recently, however, *systems theory* (sometimes *system theory*) has been put forward as representing a framework of more than limited usefulness in each of these situations and others; indeed, the case for systems theory is not just that it contains lessons applicable to all aspects of social work, but of validity throughout society. It will be argued here that, although the term *systems theory* is perhaps over-ambitious (a preferable one is *systems thinking*) the ideas which have emerged from the systems literature are valuable both to the social work practitioner as he plans his programme of intervention with the client and to the social work administrator whose focus of attention is increasingly on strategic planning and on the need to maintain dynamic control over the relationship between his department's objectives and resources on the one hand and the demands of its environment on the other.

In this third part, reference will be made, *en passant,* to the Support Project and to the volunteers who were for the most part engaged in providing general family support. Some one hundred were recruited overall, but only one-third operated for twelve months or longer. This small group of volunteers may seem a far cry from the thousands of professional social workers and ancillaries and the heavily capitalised residential sector that together make up the welfare state's provision of personal social services; but the simplicity of the model provides a useful and relevant context within which some elements of systems thinking can be explored; where it becomes necessary, the wider spectrum of the social services will be drawn in, but it is argued that the Support Project is quite suitable to provide illustrative material for an understanding of both the strengths and weaknesses of systems theory. Indeed, much of the previous literature relevant to systems theory is excessively abstruse and there is much to be said for trying to relate complex ideas about systems to simple aspects of social reality; after all, the main objective of systems theory is to provide a conceptual framework within which the multi-dimensional qualities of social relations can be studied and understood. There isn't much point in learning about systems theory unless it helps us to make sense out of interactions which had previously been ignored or which had defied analysis.

It has to be acknowledged that social work writers to date have failed to take us very far. Hearn (1958) and Janchill (1969) are the best-known early references to the attractions of systems theory for social work, and more recently Goldstein, Kahn, Mullen and Dumpson, and Pincus and Minahan have made repeated use of the term *system* and have lent emphasis to the need to clarify its meaning and its potential contribution. The student embarking upon such a task of clarification might look to the professional literature in vain; like Meyer (1972) he may well conclude that it is 'a pretentious term at best', or, with Sainsbury (1974), say that the 'systems approach suffers at present from being newly fashionable, from the risks of gimmickry and from its attendant jargon'. Even if that were the initial reaction—and there would be some justification for it—it does not follow that the ideas which have led these writers to espouse aspects of systems theory are worthless or that more carefully tested they might not become of practical value to the profession.

The best brief introduction to systems theory's potential usefulness comes in the contributions made by Carol Meyer to Kahn (1973) and to Mullen and Dumpson (1972), and the value of these pieces derives, as always in good academic writing, from the questioning approach she adopts. In one of these essays (op. cit., pp. 185-7) she pin-points three of the topics that will emerge as central to much of our present discussion: a) the identification of goals; b) the recognition of environmental factors; and c) the need to learn to live with uncertainty. Looking at each of these in turn:

(a) While reviewing a number of research studies, Meyer highlights the lack of precision in social work's objectives. 'What are appropriate goals for direct service practice in social work? Who determines them—the agency, the worker, the client? Is client need necessarily correctly assessed by the community? Only as we grapple with the question of goals will we achieve clarity in our specification of case-work practice.' Meyer reports the familiar research conclusion: 'client-worker interactions were demonstrated and in large measure found wanting as a major solution to deviance in school behaviour, dependence on public assistance, the condition of being a multiproblem family in a socioeconomically deprived area, and the state of unfulfilled promise', and she says that we must ask if case-work has promised more than it can offer. Meyer is quite clear that the business of social work is not with achieving change, nor cure, nor control, but with giving help. 'If we choose the helping rather than the socializing goal, then we will be freer to attend to the improvement of services—to socialize *them*, if you will'.

(b) The goals of casework are closely related to one's view of the relationship between the client and his environment, and Meyer argues that social work cannot be viewed in isolation from the social conditions which foster the problems the worker is aiming to treat. 'Is it possible', she asks, 'that we still do not comprehend the role of social case-work in the overwhelmingly complex psycho-social systems in which it is involved?' And, unusually in the literature, Meyer recognises that there are two parts to the environment in social work—that surrounding the client, of course, but also that within which the worker operates. Even those writers who have come to recognise the power of the environment over the client and the applicability of systems theory to diagnosis and assessment tend to be naively unaware that the social worker is similarly influenced by external factors; Vickery, for example in one of the few British contributions to the literature, writes as if the worker operated from a wholly independent base and many writers on community work seem to have an idealised view of the essential neutrality of the worker committed to galvanising underprivileged urban societies into action. Nevertheless even Meyer's main emphasis is on the client's environment and its significance for planned programmes of social work practice. The worker is not restricted to individual or group methods; the systems view takes into account 'the interlocking salient systems that radiate from the person', compelling the worker to operate in whatever fashion is appropriate to the client's needs. 'The anchor concept is still person-in-situation; only the systems framework has given us the conceptual tools to really make use of both sides of the hyphens instead of bowing to the situation and addressing the person.'

(c) Management craves for certainty: one of the expressed objectives of applied research in social administration is to reduce the area of uncertainty, and both planners and politicians can fall into the trap of expecting research to provide absolute answers. Social workers, in contrast, are too close to their clients' lives to share these illusions, but the theories of the past, Meyer suggests, have not been equally sophisticated. Now 'the world has opened up, loosened up'. We can no longer trust psychiatric diagnoses or moral imperatives; the days of linear cause-and-effect are over; 'we have to learn to live with generalities as best we can'. Meyer herself fails to acknowledge the origins of these arguments in systems theory, but Stein is more precise when she recognises the inevitability of inconsistencies in social work. If we try to be *totally* consistent, we shall be closing our eyes to new evidence; compromises and syntheses are the way to survive in a complex social system. 'Inconsistency is simply a hidden awareness of the contradictions of this world . . .. In so far as inconsistency is an individual attitude, it is nothing but a collection of uncertainties which conscience keeps in reserve, a continuous awareness that one may be mistaken or that the enemy may be right' (Stein, 1974, quoting Kolakowski).

Values may be absolute, but truths cannot ignore present or potential external factors. The social worker's diagnosis, his planned treatment, his committal to care, his allocation of financial aid: all are uncertain acts in a complex environment, and experience and knowledge can only marginally reduce the area of uncertainty. The social policy that aims at caring, punishing, controlling, educating is similarly vulnerable to factors beyond, far beyond, the policymaker's control, and necessarily contains within it elements of inconsistency and imprecision. Perhaps if we were to recognise this, we might become more sympathetic to our own failures, especially in the field of residential care where good intentions come unstuck with monotonous frequency. More important than anything else, perhaps, is the way in which systems theory has taught us not to put our faith in simple legislation as a cure for society's ills.

Systems theory has, then, proved to be attractive to a number of distinguished social work writers, and a prima facie case is established for seeking to extend it beyond the academic frontier in order to test out its potential contribution to practice, even if, as Meyer (op. cit., p. 160) again suggests, 'general systems theory turns out to be not a theory but a framework for viewing interrelated phenomena'. Research has demonstrated that there are serious reasons for doubting the validity of the linear model of cause-and-effect so far as it relates to most aspects of social problem situations, but it, therefore, follows that social work must somehow come to terms with the problems of analysing and conceptualising the dynamic and multi-variable aspects (properties) of the social reality within which its workers practice. In research both qualitative methods and developments in electronic data processing have brought about some movement in our ability to handle more than two variables but theory has been more conservative. At a time when it is clear that the present and future functioning of social work practitioners—be they professionals, ancillaries or volunteers—is both questioned and yet encouraged, the need for some clarification of the helping process in our society is self-evident. In order to attempt this, it is necessary to introduce a range of concepts and ideas from systems theory, many of which may be unfamiliar and even alien to some readers. However, with a theoretical framework drawn variously from sociology, biology and physics, it is quite impossible to plunge straight into a discussion of its relevance for social work. Indeed, the literature to date has erred either in that it is incomprehensible to social workers or in its obvious failure to come to terms with some of the systems concepts. In this and the next chapter I shall try to bridge the gap; two risks are run—systems concepts may be over-simplified in order to translate them into the social work situation or their employment may take us too far from the social work data. Notwithstanding the risks the effort seems worth making, especially if, in the process we are able to identify some significant issues for social work in the 1970s.

Contribution from sociology*

Sociologists have continued to debate in the twentieth century one of the central issues that has troubled social philosophers throughout history: is man a product of his society, or does he create, control and determine its development? 'Due to the historical circumstances in which it arose, the sociological perspective has always presented a paradoxical vision of man in society: man creates society, but man is also subject to his own creation. As Gouldner puts it (quoted in Thompson, 1972, p. 63):

*The subject matter of this section is discussed in the important paper by Dawe, and also in Thompson (ibid.) and the latter paper has provided the base on which the present author has built.

The modern concepts of society and of culture arose in a social world that, following the French Revolution, men could believe they themselves had made. They could see that it was through their struggles that kings had been overthrown and an ancient religion dis-established. Yet, at the same time men could also see that this was a world out of control, not amenable to men's designs. It was therefore a grotesque, contradictory world; a world made by men but, despite this, not *their* world.'

These alternative views of man's relationship with society have been expressed in the 'social system' approach which emphasises the ways in which *society makes and controls man*, and in the 'social action' approach which 'focuses on the ways in which *man constructs and controls aspects of society*'. As Dawe indicates, the social system approach reflects a concern with order: man is not to be trusted, but must be made subject to socially determined constraints; man is wild, selfish, greedy, and his instincts have to be curbed by processes of socialisation, law, punishment, supervision and control. Conversely, the social action approach expresses a fundamentally optimistic view of human nature, and argues instead that man needs to exercise control over the dangerous tendencies of society to become repressive and dysfunctional.

The significance of these alternative prescriptions needs little emphasis in a social work context. The social system approach, the concern with order, is mirrored in the greater part of social legislation which encompasses the social work profession: the Mental Health Acts, the Children Acts and the Criminal Justice Acts are all explicit about the need for society to control its deviants and implicitly involve social workers as agents of the law maintaining order in the community.

The social action approach, on the other hand, is also espoused— and usually more willingly—by social workers; clients are encouraged to develop their potential abilities, to claim their rights, to confront elements in society held to be constraining them and even to rebel against the repressive sanctions of society itself where the social worker feels these to be unjust. Thompson discusses whether the two views are reconcilable or not; conceptually it would seem to be difficult to regard them as being in any way complementary, but in practice there is little doubt that the relationship between the two approaches provides a clear indication of the political complexion of any regime. Dahrendorf has discussed (in his Reith Lectures 1974) the continuing tension that characterises an open society, and Thompson suggests that 'the problems of maintaining social order and of exercising human control over social forces are but two aspects of the general problem of securing the conditions necessary for the development and expression of man's capacities'. Because of this, he argues that 'the sociological perspective needs to be sufficiently comprehensive to encompass both types of sociological theorizing': action theory which incorporates an essentially optimistic concern for human creativity and a belief in the importance of allowing man the power to control the social world; and systems theory, which reflects the apparent need to restrict the individual's freedom, and to ensure the maintenance of an orderly pattern in society.

It would be wholly inappropriate to argue that systems theory, of the type just described, has much to offer the social work profession; and it would almost certainly be inaccurate to suggest that such a conceptual presentation could successfully be employed to analyse the social worker's role and function. However, Thompson not only argues for the compatibility of the two theoretical approaches (and hence for their possible combination in the social worker's setting) but suggests that the social system is continually affected and changed by the interactions that occur within it and the information that enters it. 'The concrete "organization" is a resultant both of actors following out rules *plus* the interactions of these actors with each other and with an environment whose constraints or exigencies are usually much too rich to be covered by the rules' (Buckley, 1967, p. 94, quoted in Thompson, op. cit., p. 72).

It thus becomes important in any discussion about systems theory in social work to clarify at the outset what is meant by the term; the conceptually pure form of systems theory in sociology is of little help in practice, because its acceptance as valid implies an immediate admission of the wholly determinist nature of society: man has no influence over the social order, so there is little point either social worker or client exercising any initiative or making any effort to change the status quo. All is as it is meant to be, and the individual is utterly subject to external social forces.

But the systems theory that Thompson acknowledges as apparently valid and that I shall describe in these pages is in fact an amalgam of the action perspective and the system approach and their juxtaposition in reality and the tension that characterises their relationship seems to be an accurate reflection of human society; in particular for our purposes it provides a helpful context within which we can understand some of the stresses and strains that affect the social worker as he acts at the pivotal point between the individual and society. There is inconsistency in the relationship, there is an unpredictable element and there are contradictions; there is room for unexpected growth and there is often breakdown and conflict: these are the dynamic qualities inherent in an open system.

General system theory

The social worker's most pressing problems, like those of the manager in local government, 'concern the need to maintain some sort of tolerable relationships between a whole lot of potentially conflicting people, conflicting duties, unforeseen and unavoidable demands on his time, changes of policy and changes in the outside world. He knows, or at least suspects, that the total situation he lives in is complex and uncertain . . . and he might welcome a more flexible and sophisticated framework of thought within which to cope with all this complexity and uncertainty' (Baker, 1975, p. 30). One of the main attractions of systems theory, as it has been developed outside theoretical sociology, is its apparent recognition of the confused realities of social life and its willingness to incorporate essentially unpredictable elements. It does not have the conceptual purity of the best sociological theories, but, as a *framework of ideas*, there is no doubt that it encourages a process of thinking in practitioners and administrators that has greater prima facie validity than many more rigorously defined theories allow.

The literature of systems theory is extensive, and many leading authors have made important contributions; but here my main emphasis will be on the approach taken by one of the leading figures in the systems theory movement, Ludwig von Bertalanffy; only peripheral reference will be made to the work of other theorists but it is important to keep in mind the necessarily controversial nature of some of the material.

General system theory—the form of words used by von Bertalanffy to identify his ideas—is interdisciplinary and wide-ranging. It is derived from, and in turn has contributed to, developments in physics and biology, and more recently, psychology and sociology. It is conceived as a general science of 'wholeness', valid for all systems whatever the nature of their component parts—electrons, cells, ants, men as individuals or in groups—and whatever the nature of the relations between them.

Von Bertalanffy dates his interest in it back to 1937 when he was working as a biologist trying to explain the behaviour of living matter in mechanistic terms; gradually he was led to an *organismic viewpoint*. Living beings had to be recognised as organised, dynamic objects, capable of growth; they do not conform to physical laws which apply to *closed* systems, systems independent of and isolated from their environment, systems which in effect 'run down' with the process coming to an end in some form of static equilibrium, the shape of which is determined only by chance.

Human systems and social systems are enormously complicated

but they are not, in any logical sense, unpredictable—though, in common sense terms, they may appear to be so. General system theory emerged from the need to conceptualise, if not to explain, the complexity of the dynamically interacting variables that affect living organisms and it can be applied in such diverse areas as the relationship of wall lichens to industrial pollution, of bacteria to antibiotics, of poor families to the offer of financial aid and of hostel wardens to unruly residents; in all these examples, a simple cause-and-effect unidimensional approach is known to provide an unsatisfactory account of the true position. (My own interest in systems theory was given practical encouragement when, in 1969, having been engaged in social work research for the Home Office for five years, I had become dissatisfied with what seemed to be over-simplified theories of criminal behaviour and naive policies of penal response. Reference to the influence of poverty, broken homes, cultural deprivation and the like as determinants of deviance was leading to policies, both conventional and revolutionary, which postulated that programmes of action, involving either social work or political upheaval, could attack the causes of crime and so produce beneficial effects for society. Social workers, perhaps more than most people, are only too well aware that such simple diagnostic assessments are rarely adequate to explain their clients' behaviour. Social work and social administration seemed to me to be a fruitful area to test out the lesson of systems theory; it might or might not lead to improvements in practice, but it could hardly achieve less than conventional paradigms had effected in areas like crime, personal relations and mental health in the public sector.)

Systems theory also emerged out of the felt need to allow for growth and spontaneous development in groups of living objects, and this emphasises its closeness to many of the more interesting recent ideas in social work—those of the therapeutic community, of client responsibility, of family dynamics and of creative movement in groups. 'Modern systems research can provide the basis of a framework more capable of doing justice to the complexities and dynamic properties of the socio-cultural system' (Buckley, 1967, quoted in von Bertalanffy, 1973, pp. 5-6). It provides an ideal framework for the analysis of what von Bertalanffy calls 'organised complexity', as distinct from the unorganised complexity that is rooted in the laws of chance and probability.

Katz and Kahn's definition of systems theory as being 'basically concerned with problems of relationships, of structure, and of interdependence, rather than with the constant attributes of objects' (in Emery, 1969, p. 90) could be applied without amendment to social work practice; and von Bertalanffy's definition of systems as 'sets of elements standing in interrelation' is of self-evident relevance to the psycho-social context of the client's life; it also, of course, incorporates the social worker.

We shall look in rather more detail in chapter 8 at some of the key concepts in systems theory, but it is worth reiterating the main points without delay:

(a) Systems theory is organismic, not mechanistic: it is concerned with growth, dynamism, spontaneous development; the constituent parts of a system are not passive elements incapable of reacting to external forces, and subject only to mechanical laws of movement; they interact with each other and with elements in other systems; no pattern of events, no process of interaction between component parts will ever be quite the same as any other pattern or process. (Hence the conventional social work riposte to the unduly mechanistic approach of much research: we deal with individuals, and you can't reduce them to statistics. You can; but, as the social worker well knows, you lose something in the process and, if you take it too far, you may end up with a travesty of the truth.)

(b) Linear causality is the notion used to explain processes by postulating conceptually simple relationships: A causes B, and B causes C. While there is clear justification for breaking down complex relationships in this way, it has to be recognised that the approach enables the scientist to represent only *a part of* the truth. In particular, it overlooks the importance of interacting relationships, and underestimates the value of viewing a complex pattern of causal relationships as a whole; the separate investigation of isolated variables is often essential and the results can be valid, but taken out of the context of the total situation, they *need* not be an accurate reflection of the truth, and can sometimes be quite false in their implications. One area where this is now recognised is in regard to maternal deprivation and its effect on childhood behaviour; much of the critique of Bowlby's early work hinges on the argument that the relationship between the two variables (cause and effect) depends on the circumstances surrounding them and it is therefore unwise to make a simple assertion about the inevitable results of separating a child from its mother at a given point in time. Moreover, as with the broken home hypothesis, it is less likely that the causal factor is the simple act of separation or deprivation than that it is rooted in the associated circumstances that preceded it or followed on afterwards. In other words, what is sometimes postulated as a simple matter of a statistical association between two isolated variables is in fact a rounded situation in which a veritable galaxy of factors may have to be taken into account. The importance of this assertion for practice is apparent, for it suggests that a social policy based on an acceptance of the validity of the simple relationship between maternal separation and childhood behaviour is likely to be, at best ineffective and at worst, damaging, if it fails to take into account other relevant factors. (An even more striking example of the naivety of linear causality, again in criminology, is to be seen in the erstwhile postulated link between poverty and theft; this too failed to take into account relevant intervening variables, such as the concept of relative deprivation—a concept which demands a systems framework if it is to be capable of analysis.) Systems theory is not tied down to linear causality but has been able to absorb concepts of wholeness, gestalt, holism. It accepts that problems and circumstances, men and groups, are mutually interdependent, and that we must accordingly think of systems of elements in interactionist terms. 'Many problems particularly in biology and in the social sciences are essentially multivariable problems for which new conceptual tools are needed' (von Bertalanffy, op. cit., p. 99). The notion of *organised complexity* helps us to explain why it has proved to be so difficult to develop successful prediction techniques in social work—with regard to foster-care, for example, or absconsion, or mental illness. Such techniques presuppose the power of linear causality as a way of explaining, and thence predicting, human behaviour. Generally speaking, only when the causal variables are unambiguous and multiple is it possible to use prediction techniques with any confidence. In other cases, too many additional variables can alter the balance of probabilities over time; and in any case, the very existence of the prediction technique can itself play an important part in either bringing about or preventing the event that was prophesied—a perfect example of the inter-actionist element at work.

(c) The rejection of mechanistic principles enables systems theory to allow for goal-seeking and purposiveness within the organisation or social situation. Thus one cannot presume that the social worker, for example, will have an undeniable or wholly predictable influence on the client; and although social work theory has paid due regard to notions of client self-determination, practice has not always been so sophisticated. In any case, it is not simply a matter of encouraging client autonomy, for, as Miller and Gwynne show with reference to residential care, the goalseeking and purposiveness that emerges may prove at times to be disruptive to the *status quo*. Hence the application of systems theory to social work does not necessarily lead to an egalitarian stance; rather does it require the participants, especially perhaps those with administrative or financial control, to clarify their expectations of the system within which they operate; systems theory, by recognising the respective power of the various members of the group, facilitates an accurate analysis of the group process; it does not make any value judgment about the appropriateness or otherwise of any particular distribution of power (although it might suggest whether or not specific patterns are viable under different external conditions).

(d) The environment surrounding the system plays a critical part in its existence, and indeed is the key to its organismic, dynamic nature. '. . . for open systems, there exists a relationship to the environment which is based on interconnection with the environment, and hence there exists an interdependence between each system and its environment' (Kremyanskiy quoted in Emery, op. cit., p. 136). Every organisation is conceived as an *open system*, maintaining itself in a continuous inflow and outflow, its components being built up and broken down; the open system is never, so long as it is alive, in a state of equilibrium (which is a static concept), but always maintained in a so-called steady state— that is, it may appear to be stable when in fact it is in a continuous process of growth, and may even be developing towards a state of increased order and organisation. The characteristics of an open system involve notions like wholeness, differentiation, growth, hierarchical order, dominance, control, competition, and so on. The human body is, of course, an open system maintaining a steady state, but so too are many social groupings: a family, an office, a student class, an intermediate treatment group, a hostel, a shop, etc. What about the social worker and client in tandem? Much depends on the power of the relationship, on its longevity and on the symbolic significance of each party to the other; in many such casework situations, the relationship may be simply too superficial, too fleeting to enable one to speak of it as an open system in its own right, although any analysis of the relationship must take into account the relevance of the *other* systems to which each party belongs.

(e) Although mathematical terms are commonly found in the systems theory literature, the value of the approach is not dependent on a mathematical model. 'A verbal model is better than no model at all . . . .. Models in ordinary language have their place. The system idea retains its value even where it . . . remains a "guiding idea" rather than being a mathematical construct' (von Bertalanffy, op. cit., p. 22). In the area of social science, we are content to aim at 'explanation in principle' (ibid., p. 35).

That, then, is a brief account of some of the main arguments from *General System Theory*—postulated as a way of reconciling the sociologist's theoretical choice between action and system, process and structure, dynamism and reification, control over society and the imposition of social order. It 'incorporates equally maintenance and change, preservation of system and internal conflict' (ibid., pp. 207-8) although it will doubtless leave dissatisfied those who see an impenetrable barrier between the pure sociology of organisations and applied organisation theory. However, social work's concern is, as always, to use such theoretical concepts and tools as emerge from the social sciences, and there is enough in general system theory to make further investigation worthwhile.

Aids to rational analysis in social work

Traditionally, social work's objectives have either been taken as self-evident or been defined in relatively simple terms; students applying for courses leading to a social work qualification often say that their aim is to be able 'to help people', thus implying that that is what social work is about. In recent years however, more attention has been paid to the wide range of roles which every serving social worker finds himself fulfilling: from correction and even punishment to community development and social reform. Many observers have found it difficult to reconcile what appear to be sometimes incompatible objectives and one of the attractions of system theory is that it allows for a recognition of conflicting elements in any social situation. However, if human interactions involve forms of organised complexity, social planning (of the kind which social administration and social work are necessarily committed to) requires a willingness to embark upon rational analyses of system elements, whether one's immediate interest is in family life, residential institutions or a social work intervention organisation. Such analyses can be used in the process of designing new systems, or they can be used for reviewing the function of existing systems. (In this section, as in chapter 8, we shall return to the Support Project in order to relate the often rather abstract ideas behind systems thinking to the concrete realities of everyday life as it is seen by the social worker.)

Two authors, Jaffe and Churchman, have each spelt out the important elements that must be taken into account by social planners and operators. By linking together their work, we find five basic elements identified: they can be presented logically but not necessarily sequentially. 'Rather as one proceeds in thinking about the system, in all likelihood it will be necessary to re-examine the thoughts one has already had in previous steps. Logic is essentially a process of checking and rechecking one's reasoning' (Churchman, 1973, in Optner, op. cit., p. 284).

Jaffe (in Optner op. cit., p. 230) suggests that the key to system design is the identification and mapping of system *tasks*, and argues that 'this is accomplished by creating a sequence of means-end relationships which link the more abstract objectives of the system user to successively more concrete and specific goals'; hence, in social work, if the aspiring students are right and *helping people* is a central objective of the profession, Jaffe would argue that such a broad, all-encompassing and possibly ambiguous objective is of little use in practice and must be reduced to more meaningful, more practical goals.

The five steps in systems analysis are:

(a) Identification of objectives and sub-objectives
These are usually structured in large part by the values and judgment of men; they reflect political, pragmatic, material or religious aims—for example the objectives of the National Front, a darts team, a firm of estate agents or the Society of Friends may be of quite different kinds (although there may be surprising area of overlap too). Objectives are not immutable—they are always liable to change during the operation of the system; for example, in the Support Project, one of the original aims was to help school-leavers into stable employment, but in practice this became a peripheral objective only. Moreover, in Mertonian terms, there may be a need to distinguish between purpose and function, between latent objectives and manifest objectives. What people say is the objective of an organisation may in fact have been replaced by another; it is this fact which leads Churchman to argue that 'the scientist's test of the objective of a system is the determination of whether the system will knowingly sacrifice other goals in order to attain the objective', and his example is worth quoting. 'If a person says that his real objective in life is public service and yet occasionally he seems quite willing to spend time in private service in order to maximize his income, then the scientist would say that his *stated* objective is not his *real* objective. He has been willing to sacrifice his stated objective at some time in order to attain some other goal' (Churchman, op. cit., p. 284). In professions like teaching and medicine, the objectives

are *relatively* clear-cut, but the social worker, whether he is operating in the FSU, a probation office or prison, a local authority department or a Salvation Army hostel, is not so fortunate; to speak of *teaching* or *practising medicine* itself implies broad objectives, but in the 1970s and 1980s, it is unlikely that *the practice of social work* is so self-explanatory.

Having identified a broad objective, there is a crucial second step to take: its reduction into sub-objectives, in order to eventually identify tasks (which emerge in the fourth step towards systems analysis—see page 98). For example, once it was decided to launch a Support Project with the overall aim of helping specially identified children and families, a large number of sub-objectives could be defined: to appoint an organiser, to recruit a sufficient number of competent volunteers, to identify the right kinds of families, to maintain the support of the headmasters without which access to the schools would be impossible, to secure volunteer-satisfaction. Failure to achieve any one of these sub-objectives would have meant at least partial failure to achieve the main objective. Of particular significance in this case, as in many others, is the importance that must be placed on the achievement of worker-satisfaction in the system; to a greater or lesser extent, in both the voluntary and the professional sector, this is a critical factor in the ultimate achievement of the client-focused objectives. Thus there is a very narrow borderline between the *bad* system in which worker-satisfaction actually becomes the prime objective to the detriment of the client, and other systems in which worker-satisfaction remains an essential but necessarily secondary sub-objective to be satisfied only as a means of achieving the client-focused end.

In this way, systems analysis requires a constant re-assessment of the balance between objectives and sub-objectives.

(b) Recognition of the system's environment
Every system has an identifiable environment. The environment of the system is what lies *outside* of it. This is not primarily a matter of boundaries: 'when we say that something lies "outside" the system, we mean that the system can do relatively little about its characteristics or its behaviour. Environment, in effect, makes up the things and people that are "fixed" or "given", from the system's point of view.' But 'not only is the environment something that is outside the system's control, it is also something that determines in part how the system performs'; in other words, environment represents *constraints* on the system.

It is crucial to emphasise that environment is *not* everything outside the system. In deciding whether an element is environmental to our given system, we must ask two questions: Can the system do anything about it? Does it matter relative to the system's objectives? Only if the answer to the first question is 'no' and to the second 'yes', does Churchman recognise that 'it' is in the environment. (In the Support Project, the fixed grant awarded by the DHSS constituted an obvious fixed constraint of great importance to the system but over which it had no control.)

(c) Assessment of the system's resources
If the answer to the first question had been 'yes', then Churchman would define that element as constituting not an environment exercising constraint but a resource available for use by the system. Resources are *inside* the system, under its control, the means by which it attempts to achieve its objectives. In the Support Project, resources included the paid staff, the volunteers, the efforts of the headmasters and their teacher-colleagues, the goodwill of the local press and the support of other welfare agencies; all of these were available to be nurtured or abused by the system, and all contributed to its evolution over a short or a long period.

The conceptual distinction between environment and resources is an important one in social work, especially when we turn from the organised social work system to the client-family system. Would one normally describe the social worker as a part of the problem-family's environment or as one of its resources? Clearly the answer will vary from case to case but, in a great many situations, it is likely that the family can exercise little or no control over the social worker, and that therefore he must be defined as environmental—but only if he has significance for the family. If he is peripheral to them, he is neither a part of their environment nor a resource. In examining individual cases, the answer arrived at—whether the social worker is environment, resource or neither—is a significant indication of the nature of the client-worker relationship.

In the Support Project it took a long time, and it remained relatively rare, for families to perceive volunteers as resource-agents; the majority of volunteers seemed to keep firm control over their own behaviour *vis-à-vis* the clients, and hence remained, at best, within the external environment. (The same kind of analysis can be applied to many interpersonal relationships: for example, in teacher-student relations, to what extent are teachers a part of the uncontrollable environment of students and to what extent are they a resource to be influenced and employed by the students to their own ends?)

And again the environment-resource distinction can be used to throw light on the differences between provisions in the public sector of the welfare state and services offered for cash in the private sector: those who have money to spend can convert environmental elements into resources subject to their own control. The client of the Health Service, Social Security, Housing Departments, and the rest, perceives these organisations as environmental. They are relevant to his well-being, sometimes crucial, but he has little or no control over them and must take or leave what they offer; they are not a part of his social system, not a resource under his jurisdiction; when they benefit him, as they may certainly do, he may feel gratitude, but he will not feel personal satisfaction at having contributed to his own development. The possession of money, however, changes this to some extent: it gives the individual real influence—albeit often quite slight—in regard to the receipt of private medicine, perhaps, or over the choice of a house in which to live. Of course there may be perfectly valid reasons why private medicine or private property are better abandoned so that all are equally denied access to welfare resources and all are required to make themselves subject to the environmental allocation of facilities subject not to their own choice but to entirely external determinants. But whether or not that is so on political grounds, this analysis gives us a glimpse of a key element in the organisation of welfare provisions, universal or selected: they are environmental to the recipient but there is reason to believe that benefits will accrue if some means can be found for converting them, at least partially, into resources over which the recipient feels some control and for which he feels some responsibility. The psychology of living in a socially planned welfare state is a remarkably under-explored area; if man has little or no control over those elements necessary to his own welfare, what implications does this carry, if any, for the way in which he uses them or builds on them?

Of course, the distinction between environment and resources can be a conceptual one, rather than a physical one. In many systems, some elements may be identified with both environment and resource; the best example occurs in many different guises—in the life of the child, perhaps, or in the situation faced by the resident in institutional care. In both such cases, there are others—the parent or the residential staff—who can be both environmental in that they exercise control and are not subject to system influence, and agents of resource, in that they give benefits and are open to pressure. It is known that many authority-relationships only function properly when the agent is able to balance the two component parts in appropriate proportions.

(d) **Refinement of tasks**

Churchman (ibid.) talks of components, missions, jobs, activities—

these are all the things the system must perform in the course of achieving its objectives. For Jaffe (op. cit.), the refinement of tasks is the crucial step after moving from objectives to sub-objectives: at this point, inputs, outputs and processing can be inferred, planning can be completed, and the multi-variable organised complexity is brought under control. For example, in the Support Project, early tasks included:

(a) the organiser placed advertisements in the paper;
(b) she replied to applications received;
(c) she clarified the volunteers' role to applicants;
(d) she sent for references;
(e) she made selections from the applications;
(f) she took volunteers along to the headmasters or teachers;
(g) headmasters delegated responsibilities to teacher-counsellors;
(h) teachers picked suitable names from the school register;
(i) teachers conveyed the volunteer to the chosen family.

That is just the very beginning. In any organised system, tasks may be innumerable, but Jaffe argues that systems thinking requires their rational analysis: they represent the final step in the means-end sequence, and ultimately the achievement of objectives is dependent on the satisfactory completion of appropriate tasks. Hence the reasons for each task may have to be identified and considered. However, systems design is still underdeveloped; the early steps in system design are the hard ones, and we 'do not yet have ready-made analytic tools for the job'. The main need is to make the tasks more and more specific, continually to relate them back to the system objectives (which hopefully are clearly defined) and to relate them forward to the material and personal resources available for use, and to the environmental constraints likely to be influential.

(e) **Management of the system**
All systems are 'managed', more or less consciously, more or less successfully. Each individual manages his own personal system as it affects different aspects of his life—at home, at work, in his leisure-time. Each family-system is managed, whether it be under a patriarchal, matriarchal, democratic or any other model. Industrial and commercial systems are managed; armies, political parties and football teams are managed; so too are central and local government departments. Only relatively recently has much explicit attention been paid to the different ways in which social service systems can be managed, but it has been quickly realised how inadequate were many of our past assumptions about social work and how complex

are the variables that have to be taken into account when considering future plans.

As Churchman points out (op. cit., p. 291) most of the people who have paid attention to systems analysis like to think that their work is outside the very system they are describing; they outline the preferred process of planning logic but do not really understand how they themselves are a part of the system being observed. You cannot study a system without being part of it, however obliquely; you cannot make recommendations for action without becoming an integral part of the action yourself: nowhere is there a better, more vivid demonstration of the dynamic nature of systems theory—the theorist, the thinker is necessarily a part of the action.

Nevertheless, bearing in mind his own unanticipated effects on the system, the manager must *generate* plans for development, *control* operations in order to avoid deviations, *evaluate* the effect of the system's efforts (the output) according to prescribed criteria and, in the light of such evaluations, continually *provide for change* within the system: 'no-one can claim to have set down the correct overall objectives, or a correct definition of the environment, or a fully precise definition of resources, or the ultimate definition of the components (tasks)' (ibid., p. 292). The recognition of such imperfections in any system highlights the primacy of information (feedback) being conveyed to the manager; only if deficiencies and shortcomings are communicated to those with the power to effect changes can reforms be instituted. Hence the great concern in much management literature with information flow—especially in organisations like social service systems, where shortcomings may not be highlighted by measures of commercial output like productivity, turnover, profit, and so on.

In social work, however, the pattern of generating plans, controlling operations, evaluating effects and providing for change (G-C-E-P) is not only applicable at the level of top management, as it is in industry. For each social worker in the field and in residential care is, or is expected to be, concerned with managing the system of individual clients; I have argued elsewhere (Davies, 1972) that, in many cases, where contact is limited to fifteen to thirty minutes per week, such an objective is unrealistic: in probation, for example, the most that can be said in many instances is that the probation officer is providing a form of oversight as an end (an objective) in itself. However, there is little doubt that the employers of social workers have more ambitious expectations in many cases, and if the job of the social worker is with therapeutics, rehabilitation, corrections, reform, re-education, community development, environmental stimulation, then greater consideration will have to be given to improving the techniques employed by social workers to achieve their specific objectives. Despite lip service paid by textbooks and teachers to social work effectiveness, the lesson of most recent research is that few social workers operate efficiently or successfully when their results are gauged by measures of client-change.

Hence systems theory is applicable at the level of top management, but it necessarily requires much greater clarification of objectives in the context of the social services; it is also applicable at ground level, both in the field and in residential care, but it too demands a re-assessment of aims in social work and associated areas. And, in any case, it cannot be forgotten that systems theory, although it savours of omnipotence and omniscience, and hence tends to legitimise power relationships, none the less places equal weight on the shoulders of the client. To the client, the social worker is either an environmental constraint or a resource to be used for the benefit of his own system; client autonomy and client influence are as yet ill-developed concepts but in a welfare state system operating under democratic principles, it is crucial that they be encouraged; unfortunately, like many liberal virtues, they run the risk of undermining the smooth running machinery of the larger system.

Systems theory is ultimately, like all social theory, about the relationship between the one and the many, between man and society, between the minority and the majority, between the deviant and the conformist. It is a helpful tool both for management, social work practice, and sociological theory; but it does not resolve the perpetual political issues of freedom and human rights.

Chapter eight

Language of systems theory

Introduction

The exploration of systems theory carried out in chapter 7 enables us to draw together seven points which highlight its attraction to those involved in the continuing debate about social work's role in modern society; it does not and cannot resolve all the issues that often seem so perplexing, but it casts doubt on some of the more naive dogmas that characterise the social work literature, and it compels practitioners and administrators to bear in mind the complex variables that impinge on even their most modest aspirations.

(a) Systems theory confirms the psycho-social focus of social work, but it accords greater emphasis to the contemporary environment as both an enabling and a constraining force; systems theory argues that, if social work is concerned with human behaviour and personal welfare, then it is crucial to accept as given the notion of client-in-system; only in this way can either social work or social administration plan effective programmes of intervention or development.

(b) Systems theory avoids the pitfalls of the monocausal error; it recognises, not so much the alternative notion of multiple causation, but the force of interactionist effects in social life.

(c) Systems theory precludes the necessity of committing oneself to any single objective in social work (for example, that of *change*), while at the same time compelling practitioners and administrators to undertake rational analyses of their objectives in all situations.

(d) Systems theory does not demand the overthrow of many of the most important lessons from casework theory and practice. Within a systems approach, the social worker must necessarily employ a variety of techniques determined only by their anticipated likelihood of achieving specified objectives. It accepts that there are different routes to the same goal and, therefore, that the personal qualities of individual social workers are important components in the treatment relationship.

(e) Systems theory removes from the social worker the danger of ascribed omnipotence. His professional skills, his experience, his agency identity, his personal charisma are still important to him in his work, but the primacy of his position *vis-à-vis* the client-in-system is not confirmed; the social worker merely becomes either a part of the client's environment or a resource for his selective use and his impact on the client-as-individual is wholly dependent on the success with which he can achieve absorption into the client's system. He may improve his chances of influence by removing the client from his home situation and placing him in a new system (a prison, a hostel, a hospital) but even here the evidence suggests that the client retains an impressive degree of autonomy in determining his own future.

(f) Systems theory not only emphasises the legitimacy and the essential strength of the client-in-system, it also suggests that the client might come to be seen as an influential agent within the treatment agent's system—for example, in residential care situations, in detached social work, or even in relatively structured fieldwork settings operating at a fairly intensive level (like intermediate treatment, day training centres for offenders, day care centres for the elderly, and so on).

(g) Systems theory is clearly not confined to the one-to-one relationship, but has equal applicability to group-work and community work. In these fields, as in case-work, it helps to clarify the role and function of the professional or voluntary social worker.

Seven systems concepts

Systems thinking, it will now be apparent, is not a unified body of knowledge though it draws on an accumulation of research findings over a considerable period of time; it represents a way of looking at objects in inter-relation and appears to be of particular value in social situations where agencies are seeking to exert influence, effect change or provide support according to preconceived plans. In this chapter seven concepts central to systems thinking will be presented, and, taken together, they provide a framework for further study.

Language of systems theory

Following the outline of each concept, an illustration will be provided
of the way in which it can be applied to a social work situation; all the
examples are drawn from the Support Project, although it should be
emphasised that the relevance of the theoretical material is not in any
way restricted to the work of volunteers; the challenge to the reader
that is inherent in this part is to relate the concepts and the thinking
to other social work situations with which he is familiar and to
consider whether they throw light on many of the problems and
confusions that so bedevil much of social administration and
community care.

(a) Open and closed systems
An essential distinction is drawn in general systems theory between
open and closed systems. *Closed systems* are totally isolated from
and independent of their environment; they are static, predictable
and ultimately tend towards a state of equilibrium, stillness and
inactivity. Some of the cruder theoretical models of society appear to
imply a degree of closedness, of immutable structure which absurdly
misrepresents the true nature of human relationships, and it is
obvious to all that no living organism can be represented as a closed
system: all are open systems.

An *open system* is defined as a system in exchange of matter with
its environment, importing and exporting energy, building up and
breaking down its own component parts. Although stable, open
systems are always changing, always evolving; although identifiable,
classifiable, they present differences over time and in changing
circumstances. The concept of the open system defies many of the
laws of conventional physics, despite its claimed applicability in the
natural as in the social sciences; and to the physicist it presents
many as yet unsolved problems of analysis. Little wonder then that
the sociologist, with his crude instruments and under-developed
theories, is in some difficulty handling the rapidly evolving interactions of social life. 'Open systems maintain themselves in a
fantastically improbable state, preserve their order in spite of
continuous irreversible processes and even proceed toward ever
higher differentiations' (von Bertalanffy, 1973, pp. 167-8).

A valuable discussion of open systems in a social work context is
to be found in Miller and Gwynne (1972). They use the concept of
the open system 'to help us to understand and explain the ways in
which different aspects of functioning are connected with one
another'. They talk, as we shall in the following pages, of the open
system's input, throughput and output. Organisms, including social
groups or institutions, can only survive by exchanging materials with
their environment; in industry, the materials are usually inanimate

objects but in a school or in a residential home they are more likely to be people or ideas which may themselves be a part of semi-independent systems. The materials go towards the maintenance of the open system and the output ensures further input: 'these import, conversion, and export-cum-exchange processes are the work the enterprise has to do if it is to live'. No enterprise is more than partially independent of its environment.

There are many reasons why social work groups are particularly complex in their dynamics, but Miller and Gwynne emphasise two in particular. The first is the fact that both resources and throughput are human, and their interactions are therefore capable of greater versatility and are more unpredictable than interactions between humans and objects. And second, Miller and Gwynne draw attention to the fact that the individual is himself an open system in his own right. 'He has an inner world of thoughts and feelings that are derived from his biological inheritance and from what he has learnt and mis-learnt from his lifetime of experience; he lives in an environment to which he has to relate himself in order to survive; and it is the function of the ego—the conscious, thinking mind—to regulate transactions across the boundary between inside and outside.' In the course of their book describing the sequence of events at a Leonard Cheshire Home for the Chronically Sick and Disabled, Miller and Gwynne emphasise that unconscious energy drawn out of the past experiences of each resident can be a vital factor in determining the nature, not only of each individual, but of the group of residents as a whole or of the institution as a system in its own right. Hence, they argue that, firstly, the residents' repressed memories of inter-personal experiences in the past (often extremely stressful and traumatic), and secondly, the residents' suppressed awareness of their own present position, poised uneasily between social death and physical death, both supply distorted forms of energy input which the Cheshire Home as an open system has to deal with in some way. Such energy is often not allowed for in the more simplistic models of social work and residential care or it is regarded as an aberration which sound planning and good management will overcome. But Miller and Gwynne's analysis is an important demonstration that such attitudes will not do; not only does systems theory compel administrators to pay attention to the need for clearer objectives, it also requires them to be honest about the very nature of the open systems which they have created to meet those objectives. In the Cheshire Home the input of unconscious energy from often disturbed residents was rarely predictable and it had to be considered along with other more straightforward inputs: money, voluntary help from the community, administration, the caring role of the paid staff, political developments, and so on. The unconscious forces, then, are an undoubtedly important energy input which no social work setting can ignore; of course, it is not necessarily or in all cases the most dominant input, but perhaps it is most likely to predominate if its potential force is underestimated—as in the Cheshire Home it did when it led to the scapegoating of sympathetic members of staff.

The concept of open system represents a major challenge to those critics who accuse systems theory of being static. The open system model combines action theory and the sociologist's version of systems theory; it is dynamic, and allows for interactions of unlimited influence.

Example In the Support Project, the concept of *open system* can be applied to any of the organisations involved in the Project—the schools, the MCVS, etc. It is not applicable to the volunteers *as a group;* they never met all together, very rarely interacted with each other, had no corporate identity; it could however be applied to the Project as a whole, in which the volunteers were separately recruited resources and, more surprisingly, it could be applied to each volunteer's *own* family, with a potentially significant question being: What input did *that* family-system receive from the volunteer's activity in the Project? Most obviously and most importantly for the practice of professional social work as well, the concept is relevant to the client-family: contained generally within physical boundaries, the family incorporates multiple interactions between its various members each of whom is the vehicle for continuing input and output; moreover, the Support Project itself hinges on the idea that an additional intervention in the family system—the support offered by the volunteer—will have predictably beneficial effects on the behaviour or welfare of one identified member—the child at the special school. The family is the single most dominant system in most peoples' lives (although it too interacts with and is influenced by other systems, especially the family-head's work-system and the neighbourhood systems): up to and beyond adolescence and then from marriage until, in one way or another, the individual is left alone, the family is the one system in which the majority of people participate.

The family interacts with its environment, draws resources into its range, uses them for its own maintenance and development and, in turn, contributes to the wider community; it changes, as its members age but still remains distinctive; at times when there are sudden breaks in continuity—the arrival of a new baby or an ageing in-law, the death or desertion of a spouse, the departure of a child-become-adult—the system goes through a period of crisis but, depending on the intensity of the changes, the component parts will re-form and perpetuate the system so that it remains still identifiable.

(b) **Importation of energy**

Energy is essential for the survival of any organism; the cell and the body need nutrients in continuous supply; so too the personality is dependent on a steady inflow of stimulation from its external environment (from people, from animals, from visual images, literature, sound, and so on), and social organisations cannot live unless they have constantly renewed supplies of energy from other organisations, from individuals and from the material environment. 'No social structure is self-sufficient or self-contained' (Katz and Kahn, 1969). Groups, both corporately and through the medium of their constituent members individually, receive energy inputs from a variety of sources: for example, they derive stimulus from educational and socialisation agents (hence the emphasis placed in probation and social services departments on the provision of in-service and post-experience training); they derive strength from conscious and unconscious memories influencing the members (even to the extent of reifying the past in anniversaries, founders' days, etc.); and they are enabled to continue by the encouragement and expectations of others outside. All these factors lead to a raising of morale and a consequent enthusiasm for the activities of the group; they lead to a pride in membership, and a consequent demand by non-members to be admitted; they lead to an unquestioning acceptance of the group's norms; and they lead to individuals within the system making adaptive and creative contributions to the group's development. All these are the visible signs of a system that remains alive, that remains open; they may not be, and often are not, always present together but only when all are absent will the system die and the component parts drift apart.

Vickery (1974) presents a family case-study within a systems framework; she describes the circumstances surrounding a mother of four who is being treated for depression at a psychiatric outpatient clinic. She and her family appear to be isolated within the community. 'If Mrs X were living in a bright, cheerful neighbourhood among people who were outgoing and friendly, the social worker might take the view that Mrs X's depression stemmed from intra- and inter-personal conflicts and inadequacies. However the lack of rewarding experiences to be derived from people outside the family means that the family X is deprived of sufficient positive transactions with their environment for the maintenance of psychosocial health.'

Vickery rightly does not exclude the possibility that the problems may be quite independent of the environment, though it seems unlikely. But none the less she uses the case to demonstrate that social workers need to give far greater weight to ways in which they might intervene in community social systems in such a way as to benefit the family systems whose survival and welfare depend on adequate inputs from outside. It may be, says Vickery, that the community worker would view the impoverished community 'as a client-system in its own right'. But a family worker might retain a focus on Mrs X and her family, and intervene in the community as a way of influencing indirectly the welfare of the family. 'It is easy to see how social group work with Mrs X . . . might be the method of choice and that it might be more effective if based on a social goal rather than a remedial model. Becoming a member of a residents' association or a play group scheme might do more to relieve Mrs X's depression than several hours of social work interviewing or even of home-help time. Both the psychological benefits of social interaction and the benefits accruing from the achievement of goals, such as improved play and leisure facilities, would make a contribution to this family's well-being. This does not imply that domiciliary services and a relationship with a social worker might not be an essential bridge in helping Mrs X to transfer from her role as "patient" to that of active group member.'

The fact that many questions are necessarily begged in Vickery's analysis—for example, the fact that even in mainstream therapeutic case-work, we are still appallingly ignorant of the ways and means by which the social worker moves into the client's system and successfully exerts influence of the kind described in the case-study; and the fact that the effectiveness of such systems-oriented techniques is much less well tested than is the effectiveness of case-work intervention in the traditional mould—does not undermine its interest and its attraction. Of course, it has to be said before indignant social workers say it themselves, the kinds of activity described by Vickery are by no means revolutionary; many an enterprising social worker in the past, as in the present, will have worked with his client in much the way that Vickery describes; but it is certainly true that such efforts have rarely been set down in writing; they are not practised on a wide scale; and the theoretical justification for them has tended to be intuitive. What Vickery is suggesting is that systems theory now compels us all to cease seeing family systems as isolated units and to try to relate our prescribed treatments to the wealth of inputs which the community has to offer. The poverty of the social worker and the inadequacy of his tools have always been matters of concern to theorists and teachers; systems theory is now suggesting that we should not look to the social worker to provide the rich input or to manipulate his blunt instruments for the therapeutic benefit of the average client but that we should rather see ourselves as enabling agents putting the client in touch with *other* riches, *other* tools which may well be more culturally appropriate to his needs; the social worker becomes a kind of entrepreneur bringing together systems in need of input and energies suitable for these needs. Of course, as Vickery concludes in her case-study, 'if social workers are to be sensitive to the need for improved transactions between individuals and the social network outside the family, at least two requirements have to be met. The first relates to the availability of knowledge about *the community* and the second to the knowledge about *the means of effecting change within the community*.' Such requirements imply radical developments, not just in the content of teaching for social work, but in the availability of valid material to be employed in such teaching, for our knowledge of how individuals effect change in the community is, to say the least, rather sketchy.

Example In the Support Project, the input is simply defined and accurately reflects millions of similar inputs provided by social workers everywhere: it comprises the physical, mental and material energy given by the volunteer to the family or to specified members of the family. Inputs included visits to the home and verbal exchanges, work carried out for the clients (for example, form-filling, telephone calls made), the provision of presents for the children, money and clothes for the family, car-rides, organising picnics and outings; words and personal contact predominated but some practical and material aid also occurred. The very title of the exercise, the *Support Project,* is focused uncompromisingly on the intended input and there was of course no thought in the minds of those planning it that it might be the schools or the volunteers or the MCVS that would be receiving the support (although each might well have derived benefit from the Project indirectly). The process was envisaged as a one-way process—the provision of energy for those deficient in it.

(c) Throughput

'Open systems transform the energy available to them' (Katz and Kahn, op. cit.). The body converts food into heat and action, chemical and electrical stimulation into sensory qualities and information into thought patterns. So, too, does the family, the group or an organisation convert energy input into forms which it considers more suitable to its needs: just so does the problem family of folklore convert its new bath into a coal bunker and just so does the client in the after-care office convert the offer of a chat by the probation officer into a ticket for the Salvation Army (Silverman and Chapman, 1971); but so do social workers convert new legislation into practice which conforms to their cultural norms, and so too do all people convert earned or unearned income into items of expenditure which represent the desired throughput for their own personal system. (Indeed it is significant that money is one of the most neutral of all inputs in that the recipient is almost completely free to convert it according to his choice; but it is worth noting the occasional outcry that arises when a welfare recipient spends *his* money on purposes which are deemed to be inappropriate.)

When the input is other than money, its conversion into throughput may involve system-members in negotiations in order to identify those resource-elements which the system can call on; for if the energy on offer (say, the well-intentioned *bonhomie* of a Lady Bountiful) is not convertible, it may be of no value and there cannot then be any effective throughput no matter what the intention of the agent responsible for the input of energy; alternatively, the system may sample the input to see how adaptable it proves to be, for once it is absorbed into the system, it may well become an integral part of that system and then become subject to the processes of interaction that characterise any system on the inside; but that requires that the energy input is willing to be so absorbed, is willing to become a part of the inner system.

Example In the Support Project the throughput is the use made by the family of the volunteer's presence and his offers of help. Maybe the clothes are the wrong size, so the family receives them, then throws them away; or maybe they are altered by the mother and worn by the children. Perhaps the volunteer is kept on the doorstep and her words remain wholly irrelevant to the family's condition; or maybe she is radically accepted as an integral part of the family system, exerting real influence and having an effect on behaviour, feelings and events both in the here-and-now and in the future. Even in cases where the volunteer may feel that she is not accepted by the family and where the family describes her in rather superficial terms as 'a nice lady, not stuck up, from the school, who comes down now and again to see how we're getting on', it may well be that the input, though not converted into the kind of throughput that might have been hoped for, never the less becomes a reality for the family, and has unexpected indirect effects on internal system relationships simply because of the input-agent's presence. This might equally be true perhaps of the formal role played by social workers or probation officers acting as agents of control; in this way, even an apparently cursory casework relationship may be 'used' as a systems resource within the context of a family-in-need.

(d) Output

Output in an open system is energy of any kind generated from within the system as a result of the system's reaction to energy input—although, in reality the relationship between the two is neither direct nor linear. The energy output may in turn constitute potential energy inputs for other systems. The simplest examples can be drawn from manufacturing industry where end-products are sold for the benefit of other systems (other industries, families, etc.) thus generating further input for the producing system. Models in the welfare sector are more complex, because many of the input-output relationships are indirect, and some recipients of aid, for example, can offer only the fact of their survival and/or their grateful appreciation as outputs in exchange for further inputs; hence, in the social work profession, as in nursing and teaching, much energy is spent for the benefit of client- (patient-, pupil-) systems but the effective return comes not principally from the recipient of aid but from the input-agent's employer in the form of cash and other career-rewards.

Example In the Support Project, the complexity of the output concept is immediately apparent, for the *intended* output from the family, following volunteer-input, is to be seen as improved school attendance by the identified child, improved social functioning in the community, or even increased self-confidence among family members leading in turn to their more effective use of welfare agency resources. These are the objectives of the volunteer and the Project. But in this setting, as in many other spheres of social work, both professional and voluntary, the applications of systems thinking should show us that such expectations are naive; it is unfortunate but true that we are quite ignorant about the probable outputs emerging from client systems in receipt of given worker-inputs, although the growing volume of social work research is at least beginning to demonstrate how rarely do we achieve our stated objectives (Sainsbury, 1975, amply illustrates the point).

It is not that there are *no* outputs from client-systems—such a thing would be unlikely once the imported energy is accepted by the system and transformed into a throughput—but that they are not necessarily the outputs that fit into traditional models of what help, support, casework, treatment, or therapy are intended to achieve. In the Support Project, the most frequent family-system output identified by both families and volunteers was a feeling of gratitude and verbally expressed satisfaction; there were a small number of cases in which improved functioning was reported, but it was generally restricted to personality variables and did not extend to more tangible behavioural factors: 'the chats made me feel better'. Certainly such outputs, however modest they might seem, were sufficient reward for many of the volunteers and served in turn as inputs to maintain the momentum established. One case with a more visible output was that in which the volunteer's main input was his car; the parents used it to make journeys to their son away at a residential special school; and the output was therefore the more

111

frequent visits that they paid to their son than would otherwise have been the case.

(e) Systems as cycles of events/feedback

Feedback is one of the terms most commonly associated with systems theory but it is none the less criticised by von Bertalanffy for its static, mechanistic qualities. The best example of a feedback process is to be seen in a thermostat mechanism within a heating system: fuel-inputs are burnt, the temperature rises to a given point, the thermostat switches off the flow of fuel, the temperature falls and the thermostat switches on the fuel-supply once again.

However even if the *feedback* concept has shortcomings when employed within open systems, the notion of positive and negative responses is of value within the broader perspective of cyclical interactions. Systems, as dynamic organs, are constantly in interaction with other systems and especially with those systems that make up their own environment. 'The product exported into the environment furnishes the sources of energy for the repetition of the cycle of activities'; or, in the language of cybernetics, it provides positive feedback. Alternatively a failure to convert input into an appropriate end-product will tend to lead to a breakdown in the cycle of events, a cessation of the interactional process; it indicates negative feedback.

Example In some of the Support Project's cases, the families conveyed to the volunteers their rejection of the proffered help, not usually by saying 'go away', but by their disinterest, their coolness, their formality, their failure to respond to requests or invitations; the volunteers were thus given negative feedback and quickly withdrew, sometimes from the Project altogether; they could not continue because of their failure to establish a satisfactory cycle of interactions. In other cases the volunteers provided input, the families accepted it, used it as seemed appropriate to their needs, and were privately or explicitly glad of the volunteer's presence; however, at this point, some of the volunteers failed to pick up their families' positive feedback or discovered that, for them, the families' gratitude or improved morale was insufficient reward for their efforts and withdrew. In this latter group, it was not that the client-system intended to reject the volunteers—they didn't—but that the volunteers failed to receive the input for *their* own personality or social system that they were looking for; in particular, many volunteers (after a considerable period, and a large number of cyclical interactions) became disillusioned because they had looked for, hoped for and expected much more radical changes in the family-systems than had occurred. Hence, on a reality level, they were receiving positive feedback out of the family-system's response to their efforts and had they come to terms with the limited objectives inherent in their role, there was no reason why the process of interaction should not continue indefinitely; but, because of their unrealistic expectations, they had developed a fantasised model of their effect on families with the result that they interpreted positive feedback in negative terms; hence, the failure to achieve exaggerated objectives (reduction of truanting, improved job performance, better marital relations, etc.) became negative feedback in the volunteer's eyes, despite the fact that it was perceived as positive feedback in the client's.

A critical finding from the Support Project, and one which has obvious application to the use of volunteers generally, as well as relevance to professional social work too, is this: the continuation of the relationship between volunteer and client seemed to be dependent on *both* parties receiving enough positive feedback to maintain the cycle of inter-actions. Each party could break off the relationship; each could look for changes in the other's performance so as to improve the level of his satisfaction; but each could refuse to change, such refusal almost certainly constituting negative feedback with a consequent breach in the relationship. The longer the pattern continued, the more the volunteer might be drawn in to the family-system, and the less he would be isolated in the external environment; the closest interactions of all were to be found in those cases where one or more members of the family-system were also drawn tentatively and briefly into the volunteer's own family-system. This step was frequently interpreted by clients as the most vivid form of positive feedback they could ask for from the volunteer.

(f) Steady state

'In the open system, continuous decay and synthesis is so regulated that the organism is maintained approximately constant in a so-called steady state. This is one fundamental mystery of living systems' (von Bertalanffy, 1973, p. 165). And it is argued that this principle, which is most obviously applicable to the human body, is also relevant to social systems. The open system is self-regulating; it maintains itself in a dynamic equilibrium. Any disturbance from the environment tends to be counteracted; but if it persists then such disturbance can lead to adaptations within the system and the establishment of a new steady state. Unlike the more mechanistic concepts of equilibrium or homeostasis, the notion of steady state allows for growth, for transition towards a higher order, more organisation, greater heterogeneity.

If the concept is valid, it has obvious implications for social work intervention and would seem to provide a theoretical explanation for much recent research evidence about the difficulty of making inroads on the client's situation. The idea of steady state also lends credence to the argument that social workers must beware of assuming that even the most deviant of clients is necessarily in some disorganised (anomic) social situation or that families failing to conform to a hypothesised conventional norm are necessarily in need of therapeutic intervention, for even in such apparently extreme instances a steady state may exist which will be superior to any externally imposed alternative that the social worker may be able to arrange. Thus the concept links up both with deviancy theory in sociology and with the work of the Institute of Marital Studies in social work, and sounds a note of caution for the therapeutic practitioner.

Example   The evidence from the Support Project suggested that volunteers had little impact on the total situation of the families to which they were allocated, despite the intensive efforts that some of them made. Those who came closest to being absorbed into the client-system exercised the greatest influence therein; but conversely those whose influence appeared to be potentially the most disruptive (i.e. the most radical in terms of the client's cultural perspective) were met by an insurmountable barrier that precluded them from affecting the family's steady state in any way. It might therefore be suggested that the client's system is open to influence by the social worker only when he comes to be perceived as a part of that system—a rare occurrence under normal circumstances, although there were some cases in the sample where the presence of a social worker—any social worker—appeared to have become an essential part of the family-system anyway, with the result that volunteers were simply absorbed into the system without difficulty. A different kind of influence might occur when the social worker employs techniques derived from his external authority, enabling him to exercise constraints over the client and his system, and in extreme cases, to remove him from it: but this is a totally different role for the social worker to play—at least, in the eyes of the client.

In a different example, the concept of steady state is crucial to residential settings in which new arrivals are imposed upon the existing system which is thereby compelled either to adapt to the expectations of the newcomer, or more usually, to exert control over him, to socialise him and ultimately to absorb him within the fabric of the existing system. It is apparent that many residential settings now make free use of medication in order to reduce the disruptive behaviour of any newcomers and so induce readier conversion and absorption. On the other hand, it is also apparent that regimes in residential care do change over a period of time as newcomers among staff and residents have influence over the system.

(g) Negentropy

Negentropy is a crucial characteristic of open systems—as distinct from closed systems—and is linked to the concept of steady state. It means simply that open systems do not tend to run down, in the way, for example, that a clockwork motor (which is a closed system) runs down. Because they are *open* systems, and constantly in receipt of energy from the environment, they are continually being stimulated into new growth, new developments, evolutionary movement. Though remaining as a steady state, the open system not only preserves its order, maintains itself, but might also evolve towards even more advanced states.

Example While, at first sight, the concept of steady state may lead to some denigration of the social worker's role (after all, if the family is immune to such environmental intervention, why bother?) the concept of negentropy is more encouraging. Every system is dependent for its survival and growth on receiving energy inputs from the environment; these inputs may not bring about change but they are essential for maintenance. Hence it is possible to argue that, provided he is offering a form of energy input required by client systems, the social worker is fulfilling a vital role in ensuring the continuation of living systems—whether they are in the community or in residential care. The analogous model would represent the social worker as a provider of basic and essential foods for survival rather than as a therapist offering cures for sickness; and this analogy would apply, not merely to preventive work but in ordinary case-work as well.

In the Support Project, the work of the volunteers can be represented as ensuring the negentropic process so long as they remained in contact with the family; of course, as an open system the client-family is not dependent on the volunteer for survival but the rationale of the Project is that the availability of a helpful volunteer will make a significant difference in the pattern of survival characterising each case. In fact, some volunteers made minimal impact and withdrew; but even among these there were some whose clients expressed greater appreciation of their work than would have been thought likely from what the volunteers themselves told us: often just visiting had been a valuable energy input for families who felt particularly isolated from other systems of community support. Where the volunteer carried on visiting well beyond a year, and in some cases spoke of having made 'a friendship for life', the force of the input and its consequent effect on the family's steady state were considerable—but such cases, of course, were exceedingly rare.

Conclusion

The language of systems theory is relatively alien in a traditional social work context, and, because it is employed in order to grapple with social interactions of great complexity, it too reflects something of the multidimensional reality that characterises interpersonal relations. Within the concept of systems, there is still room for a focus on one-to-one relations, on isolated interview or group occasions, and on the minutiae of client diagnosis; and for the worker, the identification of tasks *en route* to the achievement of specified objectives is crucial: hence, it is not necessary to think only or all the time in strategic terms. But systems thinking certainly demands a recognition in social work, not only that strategy is essential if tasks are to be both relevant and successfully performed, but also that sometimes the most obvious helping functions are wholly inappropriate given the reality of the client-family-system.

End-piece

Support systems beyond social work

Nobody knows for certain how efficient our urban society in the late twentieth century is at providing social support systems for its members but there is a strong suspicion, held by many people, that it is less so than it was in times past or than some less developed societies are now. Even the answer to the question 'What is the optimum level of support that any society *ought* to offer its members?' is unknown. Although there is some evidence of the isolation that may be experienced by the mothers of young children and the elderly, by young adults and the physically handicapped, no attempt has been made to put this into the context of either society as a whole or the local community and its responsibility for its citizens. In ordinary circumstances, people are expected to find their own support systems—at work, in clubs, in pubs, at bingo, in their families, in sporting activities, in churches, in evening classes, at discos; and, for the most part, there is little doubt that such a *laissez-faire* framework has much to commend it. But is it equally effective in the inner city as in the small town, in the suburban estate as in the council tower-block, in the East Anglian villages as in the bed-sits of West Kensington?

Neither central nor local government accept any general responsibility to oversee the provision of social support, nor to offer it to the population in any comprehensive manner. The Education Departments, through their youth service and adult education facilities, are probably the greatest contributors; public amenities, like libraries, swimming baths and parks, often provide a framework for the development of clubs which in turn offer support systems to those who become members.

But the Social Services Departments have not emerged as significant support systems for large numbers of people. The social work staff fulfil their responsibilities of resource allocation, decision-making and supervision in a sympathetic and supportive manner, but they are not seen by the majority of their clients as offering long-term support of a fundamental kind. One mother who was interviewed by us in the course of the work which led to Part two told us how she had valued the regular visits paid to her by the former mental welfare officer; these had ceased following the Seebohm reorganisation, and now she had no personal links with any social workers, had difficulty in obtaining a restrainer for use with her severely subnormal daughter and felt much lonelier than she had done previously. Social Services Departments are increasingly caught up with a small number of residual cases but few of them have yet evolved techniques for offering even this tiny minority the extensive and intensive support traditionally associated with the FSUs. When the support needs of the elderly and the handicapped are highlighted, a frequent response is to float the potential role of volunteers as being the most appropriate way of solving the problem. Certainly it is now recognised that the cost of training, employing, accommodating and supervising enough social workers to meet the social support needs of the entire population would be prohibitive unless a major political decision were taken to the effect that the state should accept the responsibility of providing professional support for all those who were lonely, depressed, alienated, handicapped or housebound.

Despite the obvious shortfall in resources, however, there is now and will continue to be a general expectation that Social Services Departments ought indeed to be meeting every identified need for support in any given community; this may be partly because of the expansive aspirations of social workers themselves, partly because of the continuing growth of pressure by politicians and self-help groups and partly because of the genuine and widespread public acceptance of the notion of a 'compassionate society' with its cardinal maxim: 'If there is suffering or hardship or loneliness, somebody ought to do something about it.'

Certainly the headmasters in the Support Project were almost unanimously critical of Social Services staff for failing to provide the support which they believed the families of their children required; there were some cases in which families with multiple problems appeared to have had little or no contact with social workers; there were others in which the social worker had changed so frequently that it had clearly been impossible for any professional relationship to be established; there were some in which social workers were referred to appreciatively but hardly any in which a social worker was identified as having become an integral part of a long-term support system.

It was in this situation that the Support Project was conceived. It was given birth because a small number of people in modestly influential positions were convinced that a minority group of families and children were in need of help. The objective was not so much altruistic as functional: the headmasters believed that at least some of the children involved presented greater problems at school, truanted more frequently, learnt less and were at greater risk as school-leavers *because* of their families' need for support. It was recognised that neither the school counselling service nor the Social Services Department were meeting the need and alternative arrangements were accordingly made.

Parts one and two of this book revealed how limited were the achievements of the volunteers. In so far as we have said of the Support Project that 'it did more good than harm', it might well be concluded that the scheme is damned by faint praise. Certainly the MCVS considered the Project expendable, for it was abruptly terminated in 1975 despite the fact that extension funds had only recently been guaranteed by Manchester Education and Social Services Departments.

There were gains, it is true; but these were exceedingly modest and, in all but a handful of cases, they were very short-lived. The lack of precise objectives—compared, for example, with literacy schemes—seemed to be an insuperable shortcoming in most cases; and the absence of any natural or rational basis for the volunteer-client relationship usually precluded the offering of support in the short term. Hence the conclusion must be drawn that the attachment of volunteers to clients *artificially* might be justified if there are clear objectives mutually agreed and understood by both parties, but that, if the aim is to offer a generalised form of support, then the model adopted in the Manchester scheme is probably inefficient and inappropriate.

How then are we to plan support systems in an open urban society whose structures are volatile, with a high level of social and geographical mobility and with little in the way of religious or political belief-systems which in other societies have often provided an ideological framework within which to offer social and psychological support?

Although the last century has seen a gradual crescendo of debate about welfare services policy, the focus of concern has been primarily on inequalities of income and wealth, on health care and education and on institutional provisions for the sick, the aged, the handicapped and the offender. Concepts of personal help, moral and emotional support, counselling and pastoral care have a strangely unfashionable air about them; but, despite the emphasis of much recent literature on poverty and deprivation, the circumstances which create the need for sympathetic support are not confined to the poor—though a lack of money may certainly aggravate the attendant stress. Bereavement, loneliness and social isolation, separation and divorce, disability, depression and disappointment, family stress, old age, community conflict: all are pervasive now as ever and none are the prerogative of a capitalist economy.

Support is clearly needed—in this the headmasters were right—and it is seen to be needed in many sectors of society. Applicants for training in social work still say in interview, as they have said for decades, that they want 'to help people'. But just as systems theory has shown us that the simple penological objective of 'reforming the wrong-doer' generally reflects an absurd misconception of human behaviour patterns, so too it leads us to recognise that 'helping'—when it goes beyond a single action—is a far more complex process than is usually imaged. The complexity of the helping relationship, moreover, cannot be mastered solely by an understanding of ego-psychology or the concept of the unconscious; it must be viewed in its social context. If we are to plan support systems, we must take account of the attitudes and feelings of the person being helped, of the social and ecological context within which the help is on offer, of the degree of intensity feasible and the period of time over which a helping relationship might be allowed to develop, of the personal nature of that relationship and of the evolving—and perhaps dominant—role of the recipient in the helping process.

Despite the widespread criticism of the Social Services Departments in local authorities, it seems unlikely that social workers will ever turn their backs on the helping role, although it is certain that they will concentrate their efforts more and more on those individuals and families at the margins of society. For the majority of isolated, deprived or suffering citizens whose need for help may be short-term or long-term, social workers can surely never be other than resource agents or community organisers. How then shall we plan for support systems of a more general purpose kind? How shall we strive for a society in which the man or woman in need can be helped to work for his or her own salvation without becoming case-work fodder or a bureaucratic statistic? Not, surely, by the recruitment of culturally alien volunteers to be imposed on a community from the outside, even though such people may have an occasional contribution to make to social welfare by drawing on their personal experience or expertise.

The truth is that if the concept of social support has validity and if there is a general commitment to the creation of systems which will meet the needs of individuals for personal help, then some way will have to be found to devise schemes which will allow and encourage natural communities to create and maintain their own indigenous

support facilities. Such a notion is not incompatible with a comment
by Carol Meyer (1976, p. 78):

> Perhaps we might yearn for a more intimate role of the family,
> the neighbourhood, or the church, or for the friendly general
> practitioner or the town sage as the person who will best listen to
> our troubles and tell us where to go to make use of the com-
> munity's resources. Undoubtedly it would be pleasant to have
> back that world, but it is quite gone, if indeed it ever existed in
> the idealised form. It is gone along with the sense of
> homogeneous community, quiet streets . . ..

For contemporary support systems must meet the needs of contemporary society—with its restlessness, its variety, its mechanisa-
tion, its phased life cycles, its inequalities, its trans-cultural
elements, and its unpredictability. And they must be designed to do
so in a way that conventional social institutions are not.

Two key elements play a part: social work and local democracy.
Joan Cooper, a former Director of Social Work Service at the DHSS,
has spoken of the need for social work to become much more a
catalyst in the community replacing family support systems with
community support systems, and Carol Meyer (1973, p. 49) also
looks to the social worker taking the initiative in developing new
support systems; he is envisaged as managing a decentralised team
close to the community and making much greater use of voluntary
commitment and self-help groups: 'We find in the notion of
equifinality that there is more than one way to achieve an outcome in
a case because each action taken will rebound upon another which
will set in motion yet other movements for change'. Even Peter
Townsend (1975, p. 230), the arch-enemy of Seebohm-bureaucracy
and social work professionalism, advocates something remarkably
similar:

> A form of group practice in which three or four general social
> workers would work from an office in each of a number of
> localities . . .. They would have some scope for specialisation.
> Welfare assistants and volunteer workers of different kinds
> would be attached to the group and would serve the locality,
> visiting the old and disabled, checking queries about supplemen-
> tary benefits, putting families in touch with information offices
> and legal aid and so on.

Certainly decentralisation serves to improve the accessibility of the
social work service to the client; but the models advocated still
presuppose an essential separation of the helper from the helped—
something which is justifiable only where specialist skills are

required, critical decisions have to be made or political or judicial authority upheld. Hence the second key element—local democracy —must be explored more actively and enthusiastically than has hitherto happened; and it needs to be attempted in far smaller units than are characteristic of local government wards. For although councillors fulfil a support role in respect of a tiny proportion of their constituents, they could not possibly function in the general purpose sense that is required and their breadth of responsibilities prevent them from offering long-term support even to the extent that the social work service manages. *Pace* Carol Meyer's warning about the danger of nostalgia, there is no doubt that it is the *parish model* which was the forerunner of the system of support-cells now being suggested; the geographical unit needs to be small enough for there to be a sense of identity, for there to be full and active participation by all residents, for elected leaders, counsellors and voluntary visitors to be known and respected by everyone and big enough to justify the appointment of at least one general purpose social worker to liaise between the community and its support-cell and the social services and other departments; the social worker would act as a consultant to the cell's officers and volunteers, would fulfil his local authority role in respect of extreme needs, but would not be expected to operate as a community leader. Even though some communities might require more than one allocated professional worker, the key support roles would, without exception, be assumed by indigenous residents and the responsibility of organising the cell in such a way that it could meet the needs of its residents would devolve solely on them.

It would be alien to the evidence presented in Parts one and two as well as to the theoretical perspectives espoused in the third, to suggest any simple solution. But the notion of support-cells goes beyond the eclectic nature of much professional social work, avoids the externally imposed action models adopted by some community projects and is both more natural and less cumbersome than the kind of city-wide volunteers project described in this book. It attempts to utilise the ideas of client participation, of pastoral care and counselling, of interpersonal support groups and of mutual aid with a view to facilitating the survival, the maintenance and development of individuals—in isolation, in couples, in families and in more or less cohesive community groups. It effectively denies the ultimate feasibility of ever being able to employ and pay enough social workers and social work aides in the local authority to meet the community's general need for social support. By implication it asserts the inappropriateness of society off-loading the full range of caring tasks, while still ensuring the provision of specialist skills and intensive care facilities where these appear to be required and appropriate. But more than that: it introduces an entirely new dimension, to the extent that local communities would be encouraged to adopt a developmental perspective with regard to all their residents, to raise the quality of living conditions in their locale, and to improve the range of facilities available to all.

The development of support-cells would not happen naturally and there would be much to be said for running pilot-studies to test the scheme's feasibility. Conscious, planned and determined efforts would be made in restricted geographical areas—reflecting a variety of residential situations—with a view to institutionalising the altruism and concern of a community for its own members without stultifying, politicising or bureaucratising it. Consideration would be given to the structures required, the roles to be played, and the functions to be fulfilled. Could all newcomers to an area be welcomed and given introductions? Could special attention be paid to the needs of the elderly and the handicapped? How could stigmatised members of the community be helped without increasing their stress; and indeed how could the community be helped to withhold the imposition of stigma? What role could the support-cell play *vis-à-vis* one-parent families? What might its function be in respect of members returning home from institutional care? How could the support-cell utilise the largely untapped resources among its retired members and others with time to spare, time which could prove to be a valuable asset when set in the total context of the community.

Of course, the problems in operationalising such a proposal are legion, and the biggest question-mark hangs over the question of whether it could be achieved in an ideological vacuum. Hitherto such schemes have only been attempted in the wake of political revolution or religious faith; the advocacy of such a scheme in the urban West would depend on its suitability for a liberal or social democracy. A support-cell scheme is needed, however, because without it the individual manifestations of our urban malaise are likely to worsen, the alienation of isolated individuals from the community will continue, the impossible pressures on an ever-growing army of social work employees will become uncontrollable, while the effectiveness of their remedial interventions will remain disappointing.

Already universities and colleges, some schools and industrial firms make counselling facilities available for their students or employees; but the recipients of such a service are the privileged few and those most at risk are unlikely to be affected; in any case, such schemes are not generally based on notions of local democracy. The idea of a support-cell for every citizen can only be tested if it is espoused as a conscious policy, if it is adopted without pretentious-ness but with a genuine desire to resurrect the concept of a community—however volatile—caring for its own, and if there is recognition of the need to embrace a developmental perspective in an open system.

To legislate for, to administer and to practice social work in an uncertain world are impossible tasks. But to care for one's fellows, to support the needy, and to befriend the stranger are human requirements no less important now than in the past. All the more shameful then that we have never recently considered how we can create a framework for the performance of these tasks other than by the employment of more and more appointed professionals.

Social work and social workers have a crucial part to play in the evolution of support systems, but they can never replace the basic range of resources and facilities which must remain indigenous to society *per se.*

Bibliography

Aves Report (1969), *The Voluntary Worker and the Social Services*, Allen & Unwin.

Baker, R. J. S. (1975), 'Systems theory and local government', *Local Government Studies*, January, pp. 21-35.

Bertalanffy, L. von (1973), *General System Theory*, Penguin Books.

Bowlby, John (1953), *Child Care and the Growth of Love*, Penguin Books.

Buckley, Walter (1967), *Sociology and Modern System Theory*, Prentice-Hall.

Churchman, C. W. (1973), 'Systems', in S. L. Optner (1973). pp. 283-293.

Cooper, Joan, interviewed by Mark Allen, *Community Care*, 30 June 1976, pp. 13-15.

DHSS (1974), *Report of the Committee of Enquiry into the Care and Supervision provided in Relation to Maria Colwell*, HMSO.

Dahrendorf, Ralf (1975), *The New Liberty*, Routledge & Kegan Paul.

Davies, Martin (1972), 'The objectives of Probation', *British Journal of Social Work*, 2-3, pp. 313-22.

Davies, Martin (1974), *Social Work in the Environment*, HMSO.

Dawe, Alan (1971), 'The two sociologies', in Kenneth Thompson, and Jeremy Tunstall (eds), *Sociological Perspectives*, Penguin Books.

Emery, F. E. (ed.) (1969), *Systems Thinking*, Penguin Books.

Goldstein, Howard (1973), *Social Work Practice: A Unitary Approach*, University of South Carolina Press.

Hadley, R., Webb, A. and Farrell, C. (1976), *Across the Generations*, Allen & Unwin.

Hearn, G. (ed.) (1958), *Theory Building in Social Work*, Toronto University Press.

Hearn, G. (1969), *The General Systems Approach*, Council on Social Work Education, New York.

Jaffe, J. (1973), 'The System Design Phase', in S. L. Optner (1973), pp. 228-59.

Janchill, M. P. (1969), 'Systems concepts in casework theory and practice', *Social Casework*, pp. 50-2.

Kahn, A. J. (1973), *Shaping the New Social Work*, Columbia University Press.

127

Bibliography

Katz, D. and Kahn, R. L. (1969), Common characteristics of open systems', in F. E. Emery (1969), pp. 86-104.

Kolakowski, L. (1964), 'In praise of inconsistency', *Dissent,* Spring (1964), pp. 201-9.

Kremyanskiy, V. I. (1969), 'Certain peculiarities of organisms as a "system"', in F. E. Emery (1969), pp. 125-46.

Meyer, Carol (1972), 'Practice on microsystem level', in E. T. Mullen, and J. R. Dumpson (1972), pp. 158-90.

Meyer, Carol (1973), 'Direct services in new and old contexts', in A. J. Kahn (1973), pp. 47-53.

Meyer, Carol (1976), *Social Work Practice: The Changing Landscape,* Macmillan.

Miller, E. J. and Gwynne, G. V. (1972), *A Life Apart,* Tavistock Publications.

Mullen, E. J. and Dumpson, J. R. (eds) (1972), *Evaluation of Social Intervention,* Jossey-Bass.

Nokes, Peter (1967), *The Professional Task in Welfare Practice,* Routledge & Kegan Paul.

Optner, S. L. (ed.) (1973), *Systems Analysis,* Penguin Books.

Pincus, A. and Minahan, A. (1973), *Social Work Practice: Model and Method,* Peacock Publications.

Sainsbury, Eric (1974), Review in the *British Journal of Social Work,* 4-4, pp. 461-3.

Sainsbury, Eric (1975), *Social Work with Families,* Routledge & Kegan Paul.

Seebohm, F. (1968), *Report of the Committee on Local Authority and Allied Personal Social Services,* Cmnd 3703, HMSO.

Silverman, M. and Chapman, B. (1971), 'After-care units in London, Liverpool and Manchester', in Ian Sinclair et al. (1971), *Explorations in After-Care,* HMSO.

Sparks, Ian (1973), *Voluntary Family Counsellors,* Barnado's and Channel.

Stein, Irma (1974), *Systems Theory, Science and Social Work,* Scarecrow Press.

Thompson, Kenneth (1972), *Sociological Perspectives,* Open University Press.

Thompson, Kenneth and Tunstall, Jeremy (1971), *Sociological Perspectives —a Reader,* Penguin Books.

Titmuss, Richard (1970), *The Gift Relationship,* Allen & Unwin.

Townsend, Peter (1975), *Sociology and Social Policy,* Allen Lane.

Vickery, Anne (1974), 'A systems approach to social work intervention: its uses for work with individuals and families', *British Journal of Social Work,* 4-4, pp. 389-404.

Index

Index

fairy godmother, 54
family: attitudes and opinions expressed by, 35, 51-3, 61-3; dynamics, 90; inadequacy of, 4, 8; independence of, 41, 43-4, 47-8, 59, 61; interviews with, 72; stress, 3, 7, 9, 21-2, 24; support for, 4-6, 8-9, 38-9; system, 60, 106-10, 114; view of social work, 72-5; view of the schools, 75
Farrell, C., 76, 127
feedback, 56, 60-1, 100, 112-13
frequency of the volunteers' contacts, 47
Freudian Theory, 81
friendship, 43, 46, 50, 52-5, 59-60, 62, 73
food, 40, 43

GCEP, 100
generate plans (in the system), 100-1
general care role, 9, 27, 76-7
general chat, 40, 111
General System Theory (GST), 89-94, 104
gestalt, 92
gifts, 40, 43-4, 47
goal-seeking, 92, 108
Goldstein, H., 83, 127
Gouldner, A., 86-7
group cohesion, 107
groupwork, 90, 103, 108
growth in organisms, 89-91, 93, 114-15
Gwynne, G. V., 92, 105-6, 128

Hadley, R., 76, 127
headmasters, 6-7, 9-10, 30-1, 36-8, 54, 60, 75-7, 121
Hearn, G., 83, 127
helping, 8, 24, 28, 41, 62, 66, 67, 71, 76-8, 84, 86, 94, 111, 115, 121-2, 126
holism, 92
Home Office Research Unit, 90
homeostasis, 113
home-school liaison teacher, 3, 5, 29, 36, 38, 76
home visits by the volunteers, 5-6, 21, 28, 45, 48
hostility by the clients, 51-2

identifying goals, 83-4
ideology, 121, 125
importation of energy see input
indigenous leadership, 124
indigenous support systems, 66, 122-3, 126
information flow, 100
input, 107-13
interference in the client's life, 41
interviews, research, 4

Jaffe, J., 94-5, 99, 127
Janchill, M. P., 83, 127

Kahn, A. J., 83, 127, 128
Kahn, R. L., 90, 107, 109, 128
Katz, D., 90, 107, 109, 128
Kolakowski, L., 85, 128
Kremyanskiy, D., 93, 128

Lady Bountiful, 4, 25, 38, 110
learning difficulties, children with, 3-4
learning theory, 82
linear cause-and-effect, 85-6, 90-2, 102
local democracy, 123-6
loneliness, 120
long-term care (in general), 77, 120, 124
Long-term model (in the Support Project), 28

maintenance as a social work function, 94, 105, 115, 124
Manchester Council for Voluntary Service (MCVS), 3, 5-6, 10, 35, 106, 109, 121
man-in-society, 86-7, 101
marginal role of the volunteers, 54
material aid, 40, 43-4, 47
material resources, 22
mathematical terminology, 93-4
mechanistic explanations of behaviour, 89-92, 112, 113
mental welfare, 120
Meyer, C. H., 83-5, 123-4, 128
Miller, E. J., 92, 105-6, 128
Minahan, A., 83, 128
mobility, growth in, 66, 121
money, 40, 43, 97-8, 109-10
monocausal error, 102
Mullen, E. J., 83, 128

National Elfrida Rathbone Society, 3, 5-6
negentropy, 115
Nokes, P., 9, 27, 128
non-directive casework, 47

objectives in probation, 100
objectives in social work, 94-6, 99-101
one-parent families, 22, 125
open system, 88, 93, 104-7, 109, 111-15, 126
optimism, necessity for, 64
Optner, S. L., 95, 127, 128
organismic explanations of behaviour, 89-91, 93, 113
organisational theory, 81, 94
organised complexity, 90, 92, 99
organiser for the Support Project: appointment of, 6, 10, 31; assessment of volunteers by, 20, 26-7; as the keystone of the Project, 7-8, 30; need for, 5-6; perspective on the Project, 16-31; publicity issued by, 8, 35; relationship with the schools, 17-18, 29-30, 38; relationship with

130